Overcoming Anxiety *and* Depression

BOB PHILLIPS

HARVEST HOUSE PUBLISHERS
EUGENE, OREGON

Cover by Dugan Design Group

This book is not intended to take the place of sound professional medical or psychological advice. Neither the author nor the publisher assumes any liability for possible adverse consequences as a result of the information contained herein.

OVERCOMING ANXIETY AND DEPRESSION
Copyright © 2007 by Bob Phillips
Published by Harvest House Publishers
Eugene, Oregon 97408
www.harvesthousepublishers.com

Phillips, Bob, 1940-
    Overcoming anxiety and depression / Bob Phillips.
        p. cm.
    Includes bibliographical references and index.
    ISBN 978-0-7369-1996-8
    ISBN 978-0-7369-7422-6 (Choice Exclusive)
    1. Anxiety—Religious aspects—Christianity. 2. Depression, Mental—Religious aspects—Christianity. I. Title.
    BV4908.5.P46 2007
    248.8'6—dc22

2007014301

Printed in the United States of America

18 19 20 21 22 23 24 25 / BP-SK / 10 9 8 7 6 5 4 3 2

To Dr. Henry Brandt and Dr. Jay Adams

❖

*These two men have held high the
importance of the Bible in counseling.
They have coupled sound wisdom with
a sincere desire to help people.
They have personally encouraged me and
helped me to think and grow.*

Contents

⁘ ❖ ⁘

A WORD *from* the AUTHOR

❖ ❖ ❖

*Keep your face to the sunshine and
you cannot see the shadow.*

HELEN KELLER

SOME PEOPLE HAVE SAID that when we are anxious, we are living in the future. Facing the future and the unknown often creates concerns, worries, and fears about what might happen and losses that might occur. Someone has mentioned that fear is the darkroom in which negatives are developed.

Depression, on the other hand, occurs when we live in the past. The memories of troubling events and relationships can resurface, and we can recall or relive our hurts, losses, and grief over and over. The unfairness of what people have said or done, or the situations they created, often produce anger, bitterness, and unforgiveness. Our inability to change the past and get relief, restitution, or revenge drives us into the pit of despair. The cloud of depression darkens, it lowers on us, and we lose perspective in life.

A common thread runs through anxiety and depression. These emotions seem to arise when we attempt to gain control of what we cannot always control…the past or the future. Our inability to control the events in our lives creates fears and gives rise to anger. Whether we like it or not, the desire to control winds through the fabric of our personalities.

We all want things done the way we would like and in the time we like. When we perceive that things are not going our way, we become fearful, anxious, angry, and depressed. We may even sulk, whine, or throw a temper tantrum in order to exert control over circumstances.

The way we perceive life is the key to emotional health. Years ago Reinhold Neibuhr created what has been called the Serenity Prayer. It contains a perspective on living that helps us overcome anxiety and depression.

> God, grant me the serenity
> To accept the things I cannot change,
> Courage to change the things I can,
> And the wisdom to know the difference.
>
> Living one day at a time,
> Enjoying one moment at a time,
> Accepting hardship as a pathway to peace,
> Taking, as Jesus did,
> This sinful world as it is,
> Not as I would have it,
> Trusting that He will make all things right
> If I surrender to His will,
> That I may be reasonably happy in this life
> And supremely happy with Him forever in the next.

I began counseling in 1974. Since that time I have spent thousands of hours with people of all ages and from all walks of life. Many of them struggled with anxiety in various forms and depression to one degree or another. The National Institute of Mental Health estimates that more than 40 million adult Americans suffer from anxiety disorders. Another 21 million Americans grapple with depressive disorders. Often anxiety and depression go hand in hand. They can be two sides to the same coin.

I wrote this book because I want to come alongside you if you are dealing with one or both of these issues. I want to encourage you...

- To realize that you are not alone. Millions of people are facing the same things you are.

- To realize that you cannot always stop negative or disruptive thoughts from entering your mind. However, you can change these thoughts and refuse to let them overcome you. The famous reformer Martin Luther said, "You cannot stop the birds from flying over your head, but you can stop them from building a nest in your hair."

- To realize that you do not have to depend on prescription drugs to overcome anxiety and depression.
- To realize that you can experience peace, joy, and happiness in the midst of difficulties.
- To realize that God can use you to help others. Your family and friends may be struggling with the devastating effects of anxiety and depression. You can encourage them in their time of stress and struggle.

Many people do not seek professional advice for their difficulties. They either talk to their friends or try to work out the problems themselves. Often individuals cannot afford the high cost of counseling, not to mention the amount of time it requires. Some people would go for counseling help if they knew where to go. They don't know whom they can trust. And counselors may simply not be available.

This book is a modest effort to bridge the gap between the need for help on one hand, and the high cost of counseling and the unavailability of counselors on the other. It is by no means exhaustive, nor could any book be. It is my attempt to enlighten you and offer suggestions for overcoming anxiety and depression without prescription drugs. My desire is that you would be able to move beyond just coping with or getting temporary relief from symptoms. My prayer is that you will have a change in the perception of your problems and develop a totally new direction for dealing with them. You can climb the hill of happiness and rise above the valley of despair.

Bob Phillips
Hume, California

One ought never to turn one's back on a threatened danger and try to run away from it. If you do that, you will double the danger. But if you meet it promptly and without flinching, you will reduce the danger by half. Never run away from anything. Never!

WINSTON CHURCHILL

1

The DISTURBED MIND
Fears, Phobias, Compulsions, and Obsessions

❖

*Anxiety is a thin stream of fear trickling
through the mind. If encouraged, it cuts a channel into
which all other thoughts are drained.*

ARTHUR SOMERS ROCHE

ONE DAY, DEATH WAS WALKING toward a city in a far country. A man on the road stopped Death and asked, "Where are you going, and what do you intend to do?"

Death smiled and said, "I'm going to the nearby town to kill ten thousand people."

The man said, "That's horrible!"

Death replied, "That's the way it is. That's what I do."

So the day passed. Later, the man on the road again met Death. This time, Death was coming back from the city.

The man said, "You told me that you were only going to kill ten thousand people. I heard that seventy thousand people died in the city."

Death responded, "Well, that's what happened. I only killed ten thousand people. Worry and Fear killed the others."

Horace Walpole suggests, "We are largely the playthings of our fears. To one, fear of the dark; to another, of physical pain; to a third, of public ridicule; to a fourth, of poverty; to a fifth, of loneliness...for all of us, our particular creature waits in ambush."

For Kimberly, however, it was not that easy. She could not put her finger on a specific problem. For the past six months she had been living her life with the constant thought that something bad was going to happen to her, a painful apprehension of some impending evil. Physically, she was feeling constantly fatigued. She had difficulties concentrating on anything. Even in conversations with friends she found her mind drifting off. Only when someone asked her a question about what had been said did she realize that she hadn't been really listening. It put her in many embarrassing situations.

She began to notice a great deal of muscle tension in her body. She often woke up with a stiff neck and aches in her back. Her friends and family began to notice an increase in irritability. This was compounded by her inability to get a good night's sleep. Often she had difficulty going to sleep. If that was not bad enough, she tossed and turned and woke up early in the morning. She was beginning to feel like a physical wreck.

> The direct costs of mental health services in the United States is over $70 billion.
>
> Indirect costs for mental health services is estimated to be over $78 billion. This refers to lost productivity at the workplace, school, and home due to premature death or disability.
>
> U.S. PUBLIC HEALTH SERVICE

Kimberly's performance at work was dropping. She was often on edge and fidgety. She was constantly worried about her health, her financial problems, and an increasing communication difficulty in an important relationship. She felt as if she couldn't control her thoughts and emotions. Her worries were increasingly consistent and unrealistic. She began to wonder if she was going crazy.

Kimberly is experiencing generalized anxiety disorder or GAD. It is one of the seven major types of anxiety disorders listed in the *Diagnostic and Statistical Manual of Mental Disorders* (DSM-IV) used by mental health practitioners.

Garth had a little more focused problem. He never seemed to feel comfortable in social situations. He met someone new only if a friend introduced him. He just couldn't get up the courage to approach a stranger and make an acquaintance. The closest he could come to this was to ask a salesperson a question. Although that was difficult, Garth reassured himself that he didn't have to carry on a conversation with the salesperson.

Garth's fear of meeting new people and talking with them made going to parties very difficult. Looking people in the eye, especially members of the opposite sex, was also challenging. Although he wanted to have a dating relationship, he was too shy to approach any female. He just hung around the guys and listened to them talk about sports, politics, or girls. Rarely did he contribute anything. The topics of politics, religion, or sex were too embarrassing for him. In fact, the thought of speaking in public gave him a stomachache and a dry throat.

Public restrooms created another problem for Garth. He hated to use them if other people were standing near. And even worse, if a line was behind him, functioning was almost impossible. One time, someone who was waiting said, "Hurry up!" That pressure was too much. Garth couldn't even complete his task.

Garth's difficulty in social situations did not help him at work. Business meetings and committee groups were also difficult for him. Any type of negative discussions caused him to shrivel up inside. Criticism destroyed him. Any type of tense situation caused his heart to palpitate. Meetings ranked right up there with asking for help or directions. The thought of talking with a superior at work caused him to shake. He wouldn't think of approaching his boss about a raise. He would almost rather quit than do that. It would cause too much muscle tension, sweating, and headaches. Garth is suffering from social phobia.

Individuals with social phobia often have difficulty speaking in front of others or starting a conversation. The thought of asking someone for a date creates anxious feelings. Those feelings intensify if the person is forced to confront someone concerning an issue that has any type of conflict attached to it. Any confrontation would require a great deal of preplanning.

People who experience social phobia have a tendency to...

- wear extra deodorant
- cover their face with hair
- keep their jackets on indoors
- not want to use public restrooms
- sit at the edge of a room or group
- hold a cup or glass with both hands
- ask questions to avoid self-exposure

- find it difficult to ask someone for a date
- have a hard time looking people in the eye
- hold on to objects like pillows or magazines
- pretend to be studying some object of interest to avoid interaction
- talk with their hand in front of their mouth, wondering if they have bad breath
- Speak little and not disclose much information about themselves. They may speak quickly to get it over with or slowly to carefully think out what they are saying.
- Think thoughts like these:

> *I look silly.*
> *They won't like me.*
> *I'm going to blow this.*
> *I won't know what to say.*
> *I wonder if my breath is bad.*
> *They'll find out how stupid I am.*

David Mellinger and Steven Jay Lynn, in their book *The Monster in the Cave,* mention that "as many as 40 percent of college students describe themselves as shy, and that shyness per se is not problematic unless it begins to interfere with everyday functioning or causes undue stress."

Tiffany had similar problems to Garth's. The difference was that she had stunningly intense fear and anxiety. The intense fear came in the form of panic attacks. The attacks came swiftly and without much warning. She had an overwhelming desire to escape or run away. She experienced shortness of breath, feelings of choking, and chest pain. Sometimes she felt dizzy, nauseated, and as if she was losing control. Sometimes she felt as if she were having a heart attack.

When the panic attacks occurred, Tiffany felt as if she were going to die or go stark raving mad. She was certain that the men in white coats were coming to take her to an insane asylum. Somehow she often felt as if she would embarrass herself, be harmed by someone like a mugger, or not be able to get to a toilet in time.

During these attacks, Tiffany repeated thoughts and words to herself. She clutched things like pillows for comfort, or she paced rapidly back and forth. She constantly looked around for signs of danger. For some reason, females seem to experience panic attacks more often than men.

The word "panic" derives from the god Pan, the god of the woods. People believed he made weird sounds at night in the forest and struck fear into the hearts of shepherds or travelers. His victims were overcome by sudden waves of terror and ran for their lives. That is how Tiffany felt—as if she were running for her life. The panic attacks usually subsided after about 30 minutes, leaving her exhausted and fearful that they might return.

Darby didn't suffer from panic attacks. She avoided situations where they might possibly occur. She locked herself into her apartment and shut the blinds. It seemed to be the only place where she felt comfortable. She didn't want to venture out into a world where something could happen to her.

Darby didn't want to get trapped in closed spaces like elevators or stairwells. She didn't want to get exposed to some potential danger in open fields. An animal could attack her. She did not want to be in public places, where a group of people might begin to move close to her and somehow crush her so she could not breathe. Standing in long lines or using public restrooms could expose her to disease and germs. Stampeding crowds and pushy people could harm her in a stadium. She might get trampled or pushed down the stairs.

> Approximately 3.2 million American adults suffer from agoraphobia. Agoraphobia involves intense fear and avoidance of any place or situation where escape might be difficult or help unavailable in the event of developing sudden panic-like symptoms.
>
> NATIONAL INSTITUTE
> OF MENTAL HEALTH

The thought of traveling on a bus, a train, or an airplane was overwhelming for Darby. She could barely, on rare occasions, travel in a car. She couldn't even consider driving in the mountains or crossing bridges. If Darby did venture out from her apartment, she had to have a friend with her. Darby struggles with agoraphobia.

The *Guinness Book of World Records* contains the story of a woman who developed a benign ovarian tumor. She had agoraphobia and was afraid to leave her home so her doctors could deal with her tumor. Because of her fear of going out of her house, the tumor grew to an unbelievable 303 pounds.

Carlos also suffers from intense fear that borders on terror and helplessness. He recently returned from the Iraq war and has quietly withdrawn from his family and friends. He was exposed to many traumatic battles where fellow soldiers were blown apart by roadside bombs. He had to pick up his friends' severed limbs and body parts.

A month before his tour of duty was over, Carlos was in a firefight and was hit by a bullet. It shattered his kneecap, and his leg had to be amputated just above the knee.

Since his return home, he avoids any conversations associated with what he witnessed and personally experienced. He avoids any friendships with other returning soldiers. He has withdrawn from family and community activities that he enjoyed before going to war. Carlos seems to be detaching from all of his loved ones and friends. He appears to prefer seclusion.

His family is aware that he has had a difficult time falling and staying asleep. They know he has nightmares and flashbacks of the events he experienced. He has become more irritable and even displays outbursts of anger. When any loud noise occurs, Carlos has an exaggerated startle response. When his family or friends try to talk to him about what is going on, he just clams up and withdraws emotionally. He seems to be stuck in the past. Carlos is struggling with post-traumatic stress disorder (PTSD).

Andrea's fears take on a little different shape. They display themselves by persistent thoughts or impulses. These thoughts and impulses go far beyond simply excessive worries about real-life problems. They take the form of obsessive-compulsive disorder (OCD).

Andrea constantly deals with obsessions, which manifest themselves as repetitive and uncontrollable thoughts. She talks to herself, saying things like *I'm no good, I can't do anything right,* or *I always make a fool of myself.* She is constantly counting to herself and repeating certain words

Approximately 5.2 million American adults suffer from post-traumatic stress disorder. The disorder frequently occurs after violent personal assaults such as rape, mugging, or domestic violence; terrorism; natural or human-caused disasters; and accidents.

NATIONAL INSTITUTE OF MENTAL HEALTH

over and over. Andrea has a difficult time making decisions. She doesn't believe her thinking is clear enough.

Her obsessive thoughts have turned into obsessive actions. She washes her hands over and over again. She doesn't trust her memory. She always double- and triple-checks to see if the door is locked, the lights are turned out, and the iron is unplugged. Sometimes she even reopens envelopes she has just sealed to make sure she included and filled out everything correctly.

Andrea's obsessions have turned into compulsive behaviors. She now has to touch a certain piece of furniture each time she passes, or she will feel as if something bad will happen. She has become like the little child who was told, "Don't step on a crack, or you'll break your mother's back." She has developed rituals that have overtaken her life and negatively affected her family. But she can't seem to stop them. Her anxieties have grown from small creatures to monstrous giants controlling her thoughts and actions.

We think babies are cute when they cannot go to sleep without their special blankets or teddy bears. But adults are not funny or cute when they must go through rituals of touching certain things in the house before they go to bed.

To help clarify the difference between obsessions and compulsions, remember this: An obsession is usually a mental process; a compulsion is usually a physical process. With an obsession, the individual has an idea or a series of ideas that frequently and tenaciously reoccur. The preoccupation with these fixed ideas or unwanted feelings often interferes with the normal thinking process. The individual feels mentally harassed by these thoughts.

For example, obsessive people might become anxious and worry a great deal about being physically attacked in public. These thoughts of possibly being hurt begin to overwhelm them. They envision being victims of a burglary, an assault, or a

> Approximately twice as many women as men suffer from panic disorder, post-traumatic stress disorder, generalized anxiety disorder, agoraphobia, and specific phobias. About equal numbers of women and men have obsessive-compulsive disorder and social phobia. Anxiety disorders frequently co-occur with depressive disorders, eating disorders, or substance abuse.
>
> NATIONAL INSTITUTE
> OF MENTAL HEALTH

carjacking. These thoughts fill their minds throughout the day and night whether they are based on reality or simply imagined. Obsessives begin to live their lives in mental fear.

A compulsion, on the other hand, is an irresistible impulse to perform a specific act regardless of the rationality or motivation behind it. This reaction may even be contrary to one's better judgment. The physical act temporarily releases some of the inner tension and reduces the anxiety the individual is feeling. Compulsive individuals often fall into two categories: checkers and cleaners. Two major themes seem to be common with obsessive-compulsive people. The first involves dirt and contamination, and the second has to do with aggression or harm.

People who are afraid of being physically attacked might compulsively carry a cane or umbrella to ward off an attacker. They might also carry a can of pepper spray. Compulsive people take protective devices with them when they go out in public. They constantly look around to see who might attack them. Their inner fears are carried out in protective behaviors that go far beyond those of the average person. Many people who deal with obsessive-compulsive thoughts and actions also suffer from depression.

> Approximately 6.3 million American adults have some type of specific phobia. Specific phobias involve marked and persistent fear and avoidance of a specific object or situation.
>
> NATIONAL INSTITUTE OF MENTAL HEALTH

Jermaine has many of the same physical symptoms as those who suffer from other anxiety disorders. He experiences chest pains, nausea, sweating, shaking, loss of concentration, and terror. Jermaine is afraid of snakes. Ever since he was a small boy he has been afraid of those cold, slimy creatures. Maybe as a young child he saw a movie in which someone was bitten by a snake and died. Or maybe he went to a camp, and a friend chased him with a snake, threatening to throw it on him. Or maybe he was on a hike and almost stepped on a rattlesnake. Whatever the reason, Jermaine wants to have nothing to do with snakes.

Jermaine's is fear focused on a particular object—he hates snakes. This is a specific phobia. Millions of people suffer from various specific phobias. Maybe you're one of them. Take a moment and look at the list below. See if any of the following phobias register with you.

PHONBIAS

Animals

apiphobia—the fear of bees
arachnophobia—the fear of spiders
batrachophobia—the fear of amphibians
entomophobia—the fear of insects
equinophobia—the fear of horses
felinophobia—the fear of cats
helminthophobia—the fear of being infested with worms
herpetophobia—the fear of reptiles
ichthyophobia—the fear of fish
musophobia—the fear of mice
ophidiophobia—the fear of snakes
ornithophobia—the fear of birds
selachophobia—the fear of sharks
zoophobia—the fear of animals

Natural Forces

achluophobia—the fear of darkness
acrophobia—the fear of heights
anemophobia—the fear of wind
astraphobia—the fear of lighting
ataxiophobia—the fear of falling
auroraphobia—the fear of northern lights
barophobia—the fear of gravity
brontophobia—the fear of thunder and storms
dinophobia—the fear of whirlpools
eosophobia—the fear of the dawn
hydrophobia—the fear of water
nyctophobia—the fear of darkness
ombrophobia—the fear of rain
potamophobia—the fear of rivers
siderophobia—the fear of stars

Human Body and Health

acousticophobia—the fear of noise

algophobia—the fear of pain
automysophobia—the fear of being dirty
belonephobia—the fear of needles
bromidrosiphobia—the fear of having body odor
cardiophobia—the fear of heart disease
chaetophobia—the fear of hair
coprophobia—the fear of excrement
dermatophobia—the fear of skin lesions
emetophobia—the fear of vomiting
hematophobia—the fear of blood
molysmophobia—the fear of contamination
necrophobia—the fear of dead bodies
pathophobia—the fear of disease
pyrexeophobia—the fear of fever
thanatophobia—the fear of death
toxophobia—the fear of poisons
traumatophobia—the fear of injury
vaccinophobia—the fear of vaccinations

Social Involvements

agoraphobia—the fear of open or crowded public places
agyrophobia—the fear of crossing streets
amaxophobia—the fear of riding in vehicles
anglophobia—the fear of England or things English
anthropophobia—the fear of people
aphephobia—the fear of touching or being touched
catagelophobia—the fear of ridicule
deipnophobia—the fear of dinner conversation
ecclesiophobia—the fear of church
ereuthophobia—the fear of blushing
francophobia—the fear of France or things French
gephyrophobia—the fear of crossing bridges
glossophobia—the fear of speaking in public
graphophobia—the fear of writing

gynophobia—the fear of women
hominophobia—the fear of men
homophobia—the fear of homosexuals
judeophobia—the fear of Jews or things Jewish
kakorrhaphiophobia—the fear of failure
ochlophobia—the fear of crowds
pogonophobia—the fear of beards
scopophobia—the fear of being looked at
xenophobia—the fear of strangers and strange things

Various Concerns

aichmophobia—the fear of sharp pointed objects
ballistophobia—the fear of missiles
bibliophobia—the fear of books
catoptrophobia—the fear of mirrors
chrometophobia—the fear of money
claustrophobia—the fear of confinement
dementophobia—the fear of insanity or going crazy
demonophobia—the fear of demons
dextrophobia—the fear of objects to the right
erythrophobia—the fear of the color red
harpaxophobia—the fear of robbers
hodophobia—the fear of travel
levophobia—the fear of objects to the left
lyssophobia—the fear of becoming insane
melophobia—the fear of music
merinthophobia—the fear of being bound or restrained
panophobia—the fear of just about anything
pediophobia—the fear of dolls
peniaphobia—the fear of poverty
phobophobia—the fear of fear
phronemophobia—the fear of thinking
teratophobia—the fear of monsters or giving birth to a monster
triskaidekaphobia—the fear of the number 13

Anxiety can be demonstrated through a number of physical manifestations or habits.

- tics
- doodling
- twitches
- nail biting
- hair pulling
- hair chewing
- finger drumming
- sighing frequently
- twisting of clothes
- weak handshakes
- clearing throat often
- holding of objects as a form of security
- not looking at people when they speak
- sitting with legs pointed toward the doorway
- eye movements, as if looking for a way of escape

> Fears are educated into us, and can, if we wish, be educated out.
>
> KARL MENNINGER

Are you dealing with some degree or form of anxiety? Do you have a loved one who may be overcome with anxiety? Following is the Phillips Anxiety Evaluator. It is designed to help you assess the degree of anxiety in your life. Take a few moments and answer the questions on the Anxiety Evaluator.

Phillips Anxiety Evaluator

There are 80 statements in the Phillips Anxiety Evaluator. As you read each statement, honestly evaluate the degree to which the statement applies to you. If the statement does not apply, circle the zero. If the statement does apply, try to determine the amount of influence it has in your life at

Life is either a daring adventure or nothing. Security does not exist in nature, nor do the children of men as a whole experience it. Avoiding danger is no safer in the long run than exposure.

HELEN KELLER

this time. A one would indicate a little influence, a three would indicate a moderate influence, and a five would indicate a strong influence. If you are taking the Anxiety Evaluator for a friend or loved one, simply replace the "I have been" or "I am fearful" statements by substituting his or her name. For example: "Maria has been feeling very helpless," or "Jermaine is fearful of being on elevators, busses, planes."

0 Does Not Apply—5 Strongly Applies	
1. I have been feeling very helpless.*	0 1 2 3 4 5
2. I have been dealing with a lot of sadness lately.	0 1 2 3 4 5
3. I fear being on elevators, busses, planes, etc.	0 1 2 3 4 5
4. I have been experiencing intense fear and discomfort.*	0 1 2 3 4 5
5. I feel my heart pounding a lot.	0 1 2 3 4 5
6. I find myself sweating a lot.	0 1 2 3 4 5
7. I have been experiencing shortness of breath.	0 1 2 3 4 5
8. I feel somewhat detached from myself.	0 1 2 3 4 5
9. I have been trembling and shaking.*	0 1 2 3 4 5
10. I have a hard time going to sleep at night.	0 1 2 3 4 5
11. I have restless sleep throughout the night.*	0 1 2 3 4 5
12. I have been experiencing a sort of choking feeling.	0 1 2 3 4 5

	0 Does Not Apply—5 Strongly Applies	
13.	I have been having more diarrhea than usual.	0 1 2 3 4 5
14.	I have been dealing with excessive guilt.	0 1 2 3 4 5
15.	I have been having chest discomfort and pains.	0 1 2 3 4 5
16.	I have been feeling worthless and like a failure.*	0 1 2 3 4 5
17.	I have a hard time making decisions.	0 1 2 3 4 5
18.	I have a hard time concentrating.	0 1 2 3 4 5
19.	I have been very negative and pessimistic as of late.*	0 1 2 3 4 5
20.	I find myself just sitting and staring for long periods.	0 1 2 3 4 5
21.	I have strong desires to withdraw, escape, or run away.	0 1 2 3 4 5
22.	I have been having nausea and abdominal distress.*	0 1 2 3 4 5
23.	I have frequent upsetting memories.*	0 1 2 3 4 5
24.	I have been feeling dizzy and lightheaded.	0 1 2 3 4 5
25.	I have been having an increase in headaches.*	0 1 2 3 4 5
26.	I fear losing control of my emotions.	0 1 2 3 4 5
27.	I have been very self-critical.	0 1 2 3 4 5
28.	I have been having hot flashes.	0 1 2 3 4 5
29.	I get easily embarrassed or humiliated.	0 1 2 3 4 5
30.	I have been experiencing feelings of panic.*	0 1 2 3 4 5
31.	I have had thoughts that I might be going crazy.	0 1 2 3 4 5
32.	I am afraid of dying.	0 1 2 3 4 5

0 Does Not Apply—5 Strongly Applies

33. I have been feeling numbness   0 1 2 3 4 5
    or tingling sensations.

34. I have a hard time trusting people.   0 1 2 3 4 5

35. I have a great deal of negative   0 1 2 3 4 5
    anticipation.*

36. I experience cold chills.   0 1 2 3 4 5

37. I worry a great deal of the time.*   0 1 2 3 4 5

38. I am basically a shy or bashful person.   0 1 2 3 4 5

39. I feel a lot of terror and dread.   0 1 2 3 4 5

40. I have a lot of nightmares.   0 1 2 3 4 5

41. I have been having a lot of   0 1 2 3 4 5
    heartburn lately.

42. I urinate frequently.   0 1 2 3 4 5

43. I have been dissatisfied with life   0 1 2 3 4 5
    and myself.

44. I am abusing drugs or alcohol.   0 1 2 3 4 5

45. I have a hard time getting close   0 1 2 3 4 5
    to people.

46. I avoid confrontation at all costs.*   0 1 2 3 4 5

47. I have a hard time relaxing.   0 1 2 3 4 5

48. I get easily embarrassed.   0 1 2 3 4 5

49. I often feel like vomiting.   0 1 2 3 4 5

50. I fear being in crowded places.*   0 1 2 3 4 5

51. I have a hard time leaving my home   0 1 2 3 4 5
    and going out.

52. I fear being alone.   0 1 2 3 4 5

53. I often have a ringing in my ears.   0 1 2 3 4 5

54. I have a sense of impending doom.*   0 1 2 3 4 5

55. I have a great deal of muscle tension.   0 1 2 3 4 5

	0 Does Not Apply—5 Strongly Applies
56.	I feel restless and on edge much of the time. 0 1 2 3 4 5
57.	I have had repetitive and uncontrollable thoughts.* 0 1 2 3 4 5
58.	I have had repetitive and uncontrollable behaviors. 0 1 2 3 4 5
59.	I struggle with misunderstanding people. 0 1 2 3 4 5
60.	I get startled easily. 0 1 2 3 4 5
61.	I tend to push others away. 0 1 2 3 4 5
62.	I lack self-confidence. 0 1 2 3 4 5
63.	I may be a little legalistic or perfectionistic. 0 1 2 3 4 5
64.	I feel overwhelmed by ordinary tasks. 0 1 2 3 4 5
65.	I replay conversations over and over.* 0 1 2 3 4 5
66.	I tend to push other people away from me. 0 1 2 3 4 5
67.	I feel as if I may have a brain tumor. 0 1 2 3 4 5
68.	I feel as if people will laugh at me. 0 1 2 3 4 5
69.	I worry a great deal about financial problems. 0 1 2 3 4 5
70.	I have a hard time meeting new people. 0 1 2 3 4 5
71.	I have fears of snakes, bugs, and various animals. 0 1 2 3 4 5
72.	I have a hard time using public bathrooms. 0 1 2 3 4 5
73.	I tend to put myself down a lot of the time. 0 1 2 3 4 5
74.	I have flashbacks and relive negative events.* 0 1 2 3 4 5
75.	I have been under a great deal of stress. 0 1 2 3 4 5

0 Does Not Apply—5 Strongly Applies	
76. I think about the past more than I do the future.*	0 1 2 3 4 5
77. I think it is my fault when bad things happen.	0 1 2 3 4 5
78. I have exaggerated concerns about physical hygiene.	0 1 2 3 4 5
79. I hoard and collect things.	0 1 2 3 4 5
80. I would generally call myself a fearful person.*	0 1 2 3 4 5

Number of zeros circled   _____

Number of threes, fours, or fives circled   _____

Total the number of statements that apply to your life at this time. Now count up the number of statements with an asterisk (*) that apply to you. If you count five or more, you are most likely experiencing some degree of anxiety. If ten or more of the statements with asterisks apply to you, seek out someone to talk with about your concerns. The statements without asterisks are signs of anxiety that are indicated by physical reactions, mental thoughts, or actual behaviors. If a number of them apply to you, they will suggest areas for thought and discussion. Please review each statement and note if it had a little influence, a moderate influence, or a strong influence in your life at this time. Those circled with a rating of three or more may point to the source of your anxiety.

For a long time the great Russian novelist Dostoyevsky was a political prisoner. He once narrowly escaped the firing squad by a last-minute reprieve from the Czar. He has told us that there was a small shutter in his cell door that was mysteriously opened every evening, and through it the voice of an unknown fellow prisoner whispered to him, "Courage, brother, we also suffer."

Wesley H. Hager

2

The DISHEARTENED MIND

Sources and Symptoms of Depression

❖ ❖ ❖

Depression is just a feeling of helplessness.
We are not really helpless. When we feel like
nothing matters, that's just a feeling.
Things and people do matter. When we feel like
we can't go on, that's just a feeling. We can go on.

A.B. CURTISS

THE FOG WAS THICK, and a chilly breeze cut through the warmest of coats. Even those who had lived in London for most of their lives couldn't remember such a cold day. But even in the dreary weather, many people made their way through the early nineteenth-century London streets. One man emerged from the crowd and entered a doorway. The sign above it read Physician's Office.

In the presence of the doctor, the man shared how depressed and dejected he had been feeling for some months. He opened his heart and confessed that he had been contemplating suicide.

After hearing the man's story, the doctor responded, "You need to be cheered up. You need some laughter in your life. Go to the entertainment heart of London, to Piccadilly Circus, where the world famous clown Grimaldi is making everyone smile. He will cheer you up and make you feel better."

The man sighed, "I am Grimaldi the clown."

Randy had been feeling despondent and dejected for more than two weeks. Each day had been filled with an overall sense of sadness and emptiness. Although he hadn't actually cried during that time, he certainly felt like crying. The activities he used to enjoy no longer held his interest.

Randy began to notice a significant loss of weight even though he had not been on a diet. He just didn't feel like eating, and food tasted bland. He thought his weight loss might be tied to his inability to get a good night's sleep. He had difficulty going to sleep and often woke up for no reason around 2:30 each morning. At about 5:00 a.m. he would fall back to sleep, only to be awakened by his alarm at 6:30. He felt tired and listless throughout the day. His energy level was the lowest it had ever been.

His low energy level influenced his ability to think clearly and concentrate. It was beginning to affect his job. Making decisions became more difficult. He had feelings that he just wanted to escape from everything. Even the smallest normal pressures seemed overwhelming.

Randy's self-image had diminished to a dangerous level. He felt like a failure in everything and wanted to give up. He wanted out. That was when thoughts of suicide began to enter his mind. He began thinking about various ways to end his life. He wanted to do it without canceling his life insurance policy. The least he could do was to leave some money for his family. He saw no way out from the load of hurt he was feeling.

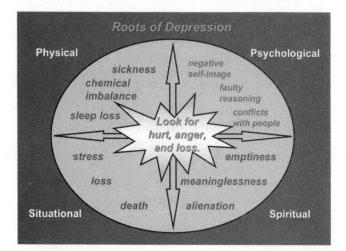

Randy was in the midst of a major depressive episode.

A complex combination of causes can lead to depression. The death of a loved one, the loss of a job, the loss of one's home through fire, or the stress of work and family life can lead to depression. Consistent sleep loss, disruption of body chemistry, and illness can compound the problem. A poor self-image, unrealistic and negative thinking, and conflicts in relationships can be quite disheartening. Boredom, emptiness, lack of purpose, and meaninglessness are discouraging. Feelings of alienation from friends, family, God, or life in general, coupled with all of the other issues, may be too overwhelming and cause the individual to want to stop the world and get off.

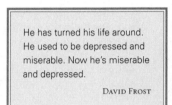

He has turned his life around. He used to be depressed and miserable. Now he's miserable and depressed.

DAVID FROST

Sonya had similar feelings to Randy but had somehow been working her way out of them. For more than a week she had been feeling better than ever. Her energy level had skyrocketed. She was filled with elation and excitement about life.

The sleep loss she had been suffering no longer seemed to bother her. Although she was not getting any more sleep, she didn't feel tired. Staying up late at night gave her time to get more things accomplished. She felt as if she could conquer the world.

All of Sonya's family, friends, and fellow workers noticed a dramatic change as she transitioned from being pessimistic to being overly optimistic. She buzzed through the office smiling and talking incessantly to anyone who would listen.

As her behavior became more bouncy, she became more interested in social interaction with the opposite sex. She had been withdrawn, but she became flirty and coy—even with her coworkers who were married. She also began to take up social drinking and was frequently the life of the party.

Sonya's family was the first to see a change in her thinking pattern. Her normally logical and deductive thoughts became more disjointed and irrational. Her judgment was not as keen, and she began to expose herself to risky behaviors—all in the course of fun, she said. Along with her newfound happiness came some unusual episodes of irritability. She exhibited a strange mix of behaviors.

Sonya's depression had made a gigantic swing into manic elation. She was experiencing what used to be called manic-depressive behavior and is now more commonly known as bipolar disorder. Just as the earth has the North Pole on top and the South Pole on the bottom, bipolar disorder refers to the opposite poles of depression and manic elation. People with bipolar disorder swing back and forth from one pole or mood to the other. They have large up- and downswings of emotions.

Sonya's behaviors had moved from withdrawal and low energy to a flurry of excitement and overactivity. Following is the Phillips Overactivity Evaluator. It is designed to help identify thoughts, feelings, and behaviors that often accompany the elation side of bipolar disorder.

Phillips Overactivity Evaluator

The Phillips Overactivity Evaluator includes 56 statements. As you read each statement, honestly evaluate the degree to which the statement applies to you. If the statement does not apply, circle the zero. If the statement does apply, try to determine the amount of influence it has in your life at this time. A one would indicate a little influence, a three would indicate a moderate influence, and a five would indicate a strong influence. If you are taking the Overactivity Evaluator for a friend or loved one, simply replace the "I have" statements by substituting his or her name. For example: "Wendy has had a decreased need for sleep," or "Carlos has rapid shifts from sadness to happiness."

0 Does Not Apply—5 Strongly Applies	
1. I have had a decreased need for sleep.*	0 1 2 3 4 5
2. I have rapid shifts from depression to anger.	0 1 2 3 4 5
3. I have been talking to people a lot more.	0 1 2 3 4 5
4. My mind quickly shifts thoughts and ideas.*	0 1 2 3 4 5
5. I have had a strong increase of activity lately.	0 1 2 3 4 5
6. I have been taking more risks.*	0 1 2 3 4 5

0 Does Not Apply—5 Strongly Applies

7. I have been more dysfunctional at home, work, or school.   0 1 2 3 4 5

8. My self-esteem has increased rapidly.   0 1 2 3 4 5

9. I get distracted easily.   0 1 2 3 4 5

10. I have had an increase in goal-directed activity lately.   0 1 2 3 4 5

11. I seek pleasure a lot.*   0 1 2 3 4 5

12. I have been fighting uncontrolled urges lately.*   0 1 2 3 4 5

13. I have had some hallucinations.   0 1 2 3 4 5

14. I have had an increase of irritability lately.   0 1 2 3 4 5

15. I have had a general restless feeling.*   0 1 2 3 4 5

16. I have been experiencing feelings of euphoria.   0 1 2 3 4 5

17. I have been experiencing a lot of wishful thinking.   0 1 2 3 4 5

18. My mind is often racing.   0 1 2 3 4 5

19. I have been doing a lot of nonproductive activities.*   0 1 2 3 4 5

20. I squirm a lot.   0 1 2 3 4 5

21. I have been leaning toward recklessness lately.   0 1 2 3 4 5

22. I have made some very foolish business investments.   0 1 2 3 4 5

23. I have been moving toward sexual indiscretions.*   0 1 2 3 4 5

24. I have been going on spending sprees.*   0 1 2 3 4 5

25. I have been binging or eating compulsively.   0 1 2 3 4 5

26. I have been hyperactive lately.   0 1 2 3 4 5

0 Does Not Apply—5 Strongly Applies

27. I have been having explosive tantrums or rages.	0 1 2 3 4 5
28. I have been involved in daredevil behaviors.*	0 1 2 3 4 5
29. I have been excessively aggressive lately.	0 1 2 3 4 5
30. I enjoy defying authority.*	0 1 2 3 4 5
31. I have a strong craving or desire for sweets.	0 1 2 3 4 5
32. I have had feelings of being superior to others.	0 1 2 3 4 5
33. I like to be in control of everything.	0 1 2 3 4 5
34. I have been staying up very late on occasion.	0 1 2 3 4 5
35. I have a tendency to be overambitious.	0 1 2 3 4 5
36. I have been experiencing surges of energy lately.*	0 1 2 3 4 5
37. I enjoy confrontation.	0 1 2 3 4 5
38. I have been fairly impatient with people lately.	0 1 2 3 4 5
39. My thoughts are racing a great deal.	0 1 2 3 4 5
40. I have been involved with a lot of unfocused creativity.	0 1 2 3 4 5
41. I have been having bizarre thoughts and ideas.*	0 1 2 3 4 5
42. I have had several migraines.*	0 1 2 3 4 5
43. I have been sensitive to light and noise lately.	0 1 2 3 4 5
44. I have been abusing drugs or alcohol.	0 1 2 3 4 5
45. I have been experiencing mental fuzziness lately.	0 1 2 3 4 5
46. I have a hard time showing affection.	0 1 2 3 4 5

0 Does Not Apply—5 Strongly Applies	
47. I feel bored a lot of the time.	0 1 2 3 4 5
48. I have been unusually happy for more than two weeks.*	0 1 2 3 4 5
49. I might have inflated self-esteem.	0 1 2 3 4 5
50. I have been very fidgety lately.	0 1 2 3 4 5
51. I have frequent shifts of interest.*	0 1 2 3 4 5
52. I have extreme reactions to criticism.	0 1 2 3 4 5
53. I am experiencing a lot of anger and frustration.*	0 1 2 3 4 5
54. I find myself performing useless actions.	0 1 2 3 4 5
55. I jump to conclusions about what people say or do.	0 1 2 3 4 5
56. I may be addicted to caffeine—coffee, tea, or soft drinks.*	0 1 2 3 4 5

Number of zeros circled _____

Number of threes, fours, or fives circled _____

Total the number of statements that apply to your life at this time. Now count up the number of statements with an asterisk (*) that apply to you. If you count five or more, you are most likely experiencing some degree of overactivity. If ten or more of the statements with asterisks apply to you, seek out someone to talk with about your concerns. The statements without asterisks are signs of overactivity that are indicated by physical reactions, mental thoughts, or actual behaviors. If a number of them apply to you, they will suggest areas for thought and discussion. Please review each statement and note if it had a little influence, a moderate influence, or a strong influence in your life at this time. Those circled with a rating of three or more may point to the source of your overactivity.

The words in the sidebar were written in January of 1841. Lincoln had been suffering from a profound mental depression for a couple of months. He had lost weight and had no desire to eat. He avoided people and didn't want to talk to anyone. He was so distressed that he constantly talked of suicide. He even wrote a poem on suicide that was published in the *Sangamo Journal*. Lincoln's friends were so deeply concerned that he might take his own life that they took away his knife.

> I am now the most miserable man living. If what I feel were equally distributed to the whole human family, there would be not one cheerful face on earth. Whether I shall ever be better, I cannot tell. I awfully forebode I shall not. To remain as I am is impossible. I must die or be better it appears to me.
>
> ABRAHAM LINCOLN

What had happened to Lincoln? Did he incur some mental disease? Had he inherited a tendency toward depression from his poor family background? Was he experiencing some form of chemical imbalance? Did the serotonin level in his brain so dramatically change that it forced him into depression? Was he on some drug that took away his ability to act and think clearly?

The answer is none of the above. The note was written to his law partner after a very traumatic event in his life.

Lincoln had met a woman named Mary Todd. Miss Todd was desperate to get married. She was seeking a husband who could possibly give her social prestige. She began dating two men, Abraham Lincoln and Stephen Douglas (the same Stephen Douglas that Lincoln would later publicly debate).

Mary zeroed in on Lincoln and pressured him to marry her. Lincoln was interested until Mary began to put him down in private and in public. She always complained about the way he dressed. She didn't like the way he walked. She thought he was awkward, and she attempted to instruct him how to walk properly. She commented about his ears (she thought they stuck out too much). She mentioned that his nose wasn't straight and that his lower lip stuck out. She also thought his hands and feet were too big and his head was too small for his body. She didn't like his bushy hair, his table manners, or his disorganization. Mary had set out on a mission to change Lincoln.

Many sources agree that Mary Todd had a very loud and shrill voice. She was a very jealous person and was prone to wild outbursts of temper. Neighbors commented that they could hear her temper tantrums several houses away. She was accustomed to getting her way, and she manipulated people with her yelling and her tears.

The closer the wedding day came, the more depressed Lincoln became. He knew he didn't really love Mary Todd, but the engagement and wedding day were public knowledge, and he felt honor bound to fulfill his commitment.

The wedding was set for January 1, 1841. Around 6:00 p.m., the guests began arriving for the 7:00 wedding, but something was wrong. Lincoln wasn't there. Mary Todd, her family, and the guests began wondering where the groom was. Did an accident happen to him?

Lincoln never showed up. Around 9:30 p.m. the guests began to return to their homes. Mary Todd was sobbing on her bed, feeling humiliated, degraded, ashamed, and extremely bitter and angry. At midnight search parties were sent out to look for Abraham. They searched all night.

The next day, searchers finally found Lincoln in his office, talking to himself. His friends thought he had lost his mind. Mary Todd's family thought he was insane. In his office, he threatened suicide, and there his friends took his knife away.

A friend named Joshua Speed took Lincoln to Louisville to live with Speed's family while Lincoln tried to get his mind in order. There Lincoln wrote his law partner that "I am now the most miserable man living."

What led to Lincoln's depression? It was the difficulty of getting out of an unhealthy relationship and all the accompanying embarrassment and inconvenience surrounding it. Who wouldn't want out of a critical and demeaning relationship? That would depress anyone.

Now for the rest of the story. Two years passed as Lincoln attempted to get on with his life. One day a woman invited Lincoln to her home. He was curious and accepted the invitation. When he arrived, who was in the parlor but Mary Todd.

Lincoln was too shy to leave, and so they talked. Several weeks passed, and Mary was again pressuring Lincoln to marry her. She told him he was honor bound to marry her and placed an enormous amount of guilt on him accompanied by many tears.

Lincoln succumbed to the guilt and pressure and agreed to marry her. Not wanting Lincoln to change his mind, she insisted on doing it right away. They went to Chatterton's Jewelry Store and bought a ring. That evening Rev. Charles Dresser married them with an impressive Episcopal service.

Lincoln's best man said that he "looked and acted as if he were going to the slaughter." Earlier that day, when Lincoln was polishing his shoes at Butler's Boarding House in preparation for the wedding, Mr. Butler's son asked Mr. Lincoln where he was going. Lincoln replied, "To hell, I suppose." So much for a happy wedding. Lincoln sacrificed domestic peace and happiness for being honor bound.

How are you doing with regard to depression? Are you feeling a little down about something? Are you feeling discouraged over a relationship? Following is the Phillips Depression Evaluator. Read through the various questions and consider how you would rate yourself in the area of depression.

Phillips Depression Evaluator

There are 82 statements in the Phillips Depression Evaluator. As you read each statement, honestly evaluate the degree to which the statement applies to you. If the statement does not apply, circle the zero. If the statement does apply, try to determine the amount of influence it has in your life at this time. A one would indicate a little influence, a three would indicate a moderate influence, and a five would indicate a strong influence. If you are taking the Depression Evaluator for a friend or loved one, simply replace the "I have been" or "I feel" statements by substituting his or her name. For example: "Andrea has been tearful, crying more, or felt like crying," or "Charles has been dealing with a lot of sadness lately."

0 Does Not Apply—5 Strongly Applies	
1. I have been tearful, crying more, or feeling like crying.*	0 1 2 3 4 5
2. I have been dealing with a lot of sadness lately.*	0 1 2 3 4 5
3. I have been feeling lonely.*	0 1 2 3 4 5
4. My motivation level is very low.	0 1 2 3 4 5
5. I have had thoughts that life is not worth living.*	0 1 2 3 4 5
6. I have strong feelings of emptiness.	0 1 2 3 4 5

0 Does Not Apply—5 Strongly Applies	
7. I have a hard time getting interested in anything.	0 1 2 3 4 5
8. I have had a recent weight loss.*	0 1 2 3 4 5
9. I have had a recent weight gain.*	0 1 2 3 4 5
10. I have a hard time going to sleep at night.	0 1 2 3 4 5
11. I have restless sleep throughout the night.*	0 1 2 3 4 5
12. I have a hard time getting up in the morning.*	0 1 2 3 4 5
13. I am sleeping more than I did before.	0 1 2 3 4 5
14. I feel fatigued, tired, and have a low energy level.	0 1 2 3 4 5
15. I have a general restless feeling.	0 1 2 3 4 5
16. I have been feeling as if I'm worthless and a failure.*	0 1 2 3 4 5
17. I have a hard time making decisions.	0 1 2 3 4 5
18. I have a hard time concentrating.	0 1 2 3 4 5
19. I have been very negative and pessimistic lately.	0 1 2 3 4 5
20. I sit and stare for long periods.	0 1 2 3 4 5
21. I have strong desires to withdraw, escape, or run away.*	0 1 2 3 4 5
22. I have had rapid shifts from anger to depression.	0 1 2 3 4 5
23. I have noticed a decrease in my sexual desires.*	0 1 2 3 4 5
24. I have been starving myself to lose weight.	0 1 2 3 4 5
25. I have been having an increase in headaches.	0 1 2 3 4 5
26. I have been struggling with constipation.	0 1 2 3 4 5

0 Does Not Apply—5 Strongly Applies	
27. I have been very self-critical lately.	0 1 2 3 4 5
28. My hands are often cold.	0 1 2 3 4 5
29. I have had some dizziness.	0 1 2 3 4 5
30. I have experienced some blurred vision.	0 1 2 3 4 5
31. I have been struggling with grief and loss.*	0 1 2 3 4 5
32. I have had thoughts that I might be losing my mind.	0 1 2 3 4 5
33. I feel a strong sense of hopelessness.*	0 1 2 3 4 5
34. I have been very irritable lately.	0 1 2 3 4 5
35. I sweat a lot.	0 1 2 3 4 5
36. I avoid people a lot.	0 1 2 3 4 5
37. I dislike confrontation and tend to run from it.*	0 1 2 3 4 5
38. I have a hard time asking people for help.	0 1 2 3 4 5
39. I think I have a distorted body image.	0 1 2 3 4 5
40. I have been having a lot of back pain.	0 1 2 3 4 5
41. I have been having a lot of stomach problems.	0 1 2 3 4 5
42. I have been experiencing a lot of neck pain.	0 1 2 3 4 5
43. I have been dissatisfied with life and with myself.	0 1 2 3 4 5
44. I am abusing drugs and alcohol.	0 1 2 3 4 5
45. I am fascinated with morbid thoughts.	0 1 2 3 4 5
46. I have a hard time showing affection.	0 1 2 3 4 5
47. I feel bored a lot of the time.	0 1 2 3 4 5
48. I have been forgetful lately.	0 1 2 3 4 5
49. I find myself provoking fights with family and others.*	0 1 2 3 4 5

0 Does Not Apply—5 Strongly Applies

50. I have been involved with self-mutilation of my body.   0 1 2 3 4 5

51. I have had poor performance at school or work.   0 1 2 3 4 5

52. I feel isolated from people.   0 1 2 3 4 5

53. I have extreme reactions to criticism.   0 1 2 3 4 5

54. I have a general stressed-out feeling.*   0 1 2 3 4 5

55. I have been irritable and bitter.   0 1 2 3 4 5

56. I have experienced slurred speech.   0 1 2 3 4 5

57. I have had repetitive and uncontrollable thoughts.   0 1 2 3 4 5

58. I have had repetitive and uncontrollable behaviors.   0 1 2 3 4 5

59. I struggle with misunderstanding people.   0 1 2 3 4 5

60. I have had some hallucinations.   0 1 2 3 4 5

61. I have experienced more accidents lately.   0 1 2 3 4 5

62. I have been cynical and sarcastic lately.   0 1 2 3 4 5

63. Others have been picking up my end of the work.   0 1 2 3 4 5

64. I have experienced or am experiencing a separation or divorce.   0 1 2 3 4 5

65. I have recently lost a loved one.*   0 1 2 3 4 5

66. I have lost the will to live.   0 1 2 3 4 5

67. I tend to push others away.   0 1 2 3 4 5

68. I have a lack of self-confidence.*   0 1 2 3 4 5

69. I feel as if people are out to get me.   0 1 2 3 4 5

70. I am experiencing a lot of anger and frustration.*   0 1 2 3 4 5

71. I have been performing useless actions.   0 1 2 3 4 5

	0 Does Not Apply—5 Strongly Applies
72. I have a hard time experiencing pleasure.	0 1 2 3 4 5
73. I may be a little legalistic or perfectionistic.	0 1 2 3 4 5
74. I have been neglecting my appearance.	0 1 2 3 4 5
75. I jump to conclusions about what people say or do.	0 1 2 3 4 5
76. I feel overwhelmed by ordinary tasks.	0 1 2 3 4 5
77. I have lost my sense of humor.	0 1 2 3 4 5
78. My forehead has been furrowed a lot.	0 1 2 3 4 5
79. I replay conversations over and over.*	0 1 2 3 4 5
80. I sigh often.	0 1 2 3 4 5
81. I feel unsupported by people.	0 1 2 3 4 5
82. I tend to push other people away from me.	0 1 2 3 4 5
Number of zeros circled	_____
Number of threes, fours, or fives circled	_____

Total the number of statements that apply to your life at this time. Now count up the number of statements with an asterisk (*) that apply to you. If you count five or more, you are most likely experiencing some degree of depression. If ten or more of the statements with asterisks apply to you, seek out someone to talk with about your concerns. The statements without asterisks are signs of depression that are indicated by physical reactions, mental thoughts, or actual behaviors. If a number of them apply to you, they will suggest areas for thought and discussion. Please review each statement and note if it had a little influence, a moderate influence, or a strong influence in your life at this time. Those circled with a rating of three or more may point to the source of your depression.

The High Cost of Thoughts, Emotions, and Moods

So far in this book we have been looking generally at anxiety and depression so that you might understand and possibly identify with the symptoms and indicators of these thoughts, emotions, and moods.

The Pit of Despair

	Mental	Physical	Emotional	Spiritual	Discouraged
Mild Depression (hours/days) **normal functioning**	self-doubt resentment self-pity	loss of appetite sleeplessness unkempt appearance	discontent sadness irritability	questions God's will displeased with God's will ungrateful unbelieving	People usually try to handle the problem alone.
Moderate Depression (weeks) **impaired functioning**	self-critical anger self-pity	apathy hypochondria weepiness	distress sorrow loneliness	anger at God's will rejects God's will gripes about God's will	**Despondent** People often talk with others to get advice and help with their problem.
Severe Depression (months/years) **incapacitated functioning**	self-rejection bitterness self-pity	withdrawal passivity catatonia	hopelessness schizophrenia abandonment	resentment of God's Word indifferent to God's Word unbelief in God's Word	**Despair** People stop talking about the problem and start taking drugs and electric shock treatment.

Suicide becomes 180-degree murder

> Fear is like fire. If controlled it will help you; if uncontrolled, it will rise up and destroy you. Men's actions depend to a great extent upon fear. We do things either because we enjoy doing them or because we are afraid not to do them.
>
> JOHN F. MILBURN

Anxiety and depression can be your best friends or your worst enemies. They can hobble your ability to think clearly or act decisively. They can rob you of the capacity to fully enjoy life. They are simply indicators that something is important to you. Something is going on in your life. They are like smoke alarms or little red flags waving back and forth, trying to get your attention and attempting to warn you of possible danger. The feelings of anxiety and depression may be based on reality or on mere fantasy. Determining the real from the imagined is imperative.

Our physical bodies have been designed by God with nerve endings that alert us to danger. If we touch a hot stove, our body is instantly alerted, and we instinctively withdraw our hand. Even though initial pain is involved, that pain is actually your best friend. It helps you to keep from getting first-, second-, and third-degree burns. If, however, I leave my hand on a hot stove and refuse to listen to my body's danger signals (in the form of pain), I can be severely burned and possibly lose the use of my hand.

> Each is given a bag of tools,
> A shapeless mass,
> A book of rules;
> And each must make,
> Ere life is flown,
> A stumbling block
> Or a stepping-stone.
>
> R.L. SHARPE

In the same way, God has given us some emotions that can alert us to danger. Anger, fear, anxiety, and depression are helpful to us if we listen and respond properly. If we do not listen, we may get first-, second-, or third-degree emotional burns. If we don't heed these emotions, we may experience severe emotional scarring.

Emotional healing takes place when we face our fears and angers. This releases a vast reservoir of hidden energy, and we create the ability to overcome anxiety and depression.

Over the years, I have seen spouses get fed up and leave each other. I have known both men and women who have lost the right to see their own children. Some families have gone so far as to disown family members.

Some people's inability to deal with their emotions has caused their friends to desert them. They have become isolated socially. Their moods have caused them to miss work, to be fired, or to be expelled from school because of their incapability to get along with others.

Divorce, broken relationships, and loss of jobs can cause massive financial problems, loss of possessions, and dependency on charity or government assistance. Some who have been unwilling or incapable of handling their emotions have dropped into substance abuse problems, imprisonment, and homelessness.

Three Major Questions in Emotional Well-Being

1. What is going on?
2. How do you feel about it?
3. Do you want to change?

What is going on in your life with regard to anxiety and depression? Are you happy with the results? Would you like to make some changes? If so, please read on. A whole new door of opportunity waits for you.

If the load of tomorrow be added to that of yesterday and carried today, it will make the strongest falter. Live in day-tight compartments. Don't let yesterday and tomorrow intrude on your life. Live one day at a time. You'll avoid the waste of energy, the mental distress, the nervous worries that dog the steps of the man who's anxious about the future.

WILLIAM OSLER

3

The DISTRESSED MIND
The Effects of Stress

❖

He who rides a tiger is afraid to dismount.

CHINESE PROVERB

THE FBI CRIME CLOCK INFORMS US that a murder occurs in America every 34 minutes. A forcible rape takes place every 6 minutes and a robbery every minute. Thefts increase to one every 5 seconds and burglaries every 15 seconds. A motor vehicle is stolen every 27 seconds, and an aggravated assault happens every 34 seconds. If that were not enough, the television constantly reminds us of war, terrorism, and the death of soldiers. We are living in stressful times.

Cassidy, however, isn't thinking about terrorism. She's worrying about whether she'll have enough money to buy food for her two children. She and Wes had a very messy divorce, and the adjustment to single parenthood hasn't been easy.

Darren picked up his check last Friday, and his mouth dropped open in shock. It contained a pink slip informing him that his company was downsizing and that he no longer had a job. He had heard rumblings that layoffs could be coming, but he never thought he would be one of them. He didn't have much money saved, and now he was sweating how he was going to pay his bills.

Mr. Carlson sat in his rocking chair and stared out the window. He didn't want to see anyone, and he didn't want to eat. There were no more tears. He had cried them all out, and now all that was left was deep loneliness and emptiness. Ten days had elapsed since the funeral. Sarah, his wife of 52 years, had passed away, and he didn't want to live without her.

Angela was curled up on the couch in an afghan her grandmother had knit for her. The doors were locked, and the television was on. She had been looking at it for over an hour, but nothing was registering in her mind except terror and anger. Her eyes were red, and her nose was running. She couldn't get the vividness of the rape out of her mind.

> A study by Weissman (1987) has found that individuals in conflicted marriages are 25 times more likely to be depressed than individuals in non-distressed marriages.
>
> ROBERT LEAHY AND
> STEPHEN HOLLAND

Rev. McKinney paced back and forth in his study, shaking his head. The hurt he felt was overwhelming. How could this have happened? The church business meeting had been a disaster. Many in the congregation had spoken harshly and bitterly about his leadership. They raised no moral issues, only a disagreement about the direction the church was going and how they didn't like his preaching. His wife was devastated. She couldn't face anyone. His children were angry, and he was afraid they would never want to set foot in another church. What was he going to do for a living now?

Mario and Alessia had a wonderful king-size bed, but they weren't enjoying it. They had rolled onto their sides, and each was as close to the edge as possible without falling out of bed. Their relationship was a disaster. The silence between them was overwhelming, and sleep was out of the question. The small irritations between them had become like bricks that had slowly formed a wall of hurt.

The Wall

Their wedding picture mocked them from the table, these two, whose minds no longer touched each other.

They lived with such a heavy barricade between them that neither battering ram of words nor artilleries of touch could break it down.

Somewhere, between the oldest child's first tooth and the youngest daughter's graduation, they lost each other.

Throughout the years, each slowly unraveled that tangled ball of string called self, and as they tugged at stubborn knots, each kept his searching from the other.

Sometimes she cried at night and begged the whispering darkness to tell her who she was.

He lay beside her, snoring like a hibernating bear, unaware of her winter.

Once, after they had made love, he wanted to tell her how afraid he was of dying, but fearing to show his naked soul, he spoke instead about the beauty of her breasts.

She took a course in modern art, trying to find herself in colors splashed upon a canvas, and complained to other women about men who were insensitive.

He climbed into a tomb called "the office," wrapped his mind in a shroud of paper figures, and buried himself in customers.

Slowly, the wall between them rose, cemented by the mortar of indifference.

One day, reaching out to touch each other, they found a barrier they could not penetrate, and recoiling from the coldness of the stone, each retreated from the stranger on the other side.

For when loves dies, it is not in a moment of angry battle, nor when fiery bodies lose their heat.

It lies panting…exhausted…expiring at the bottom of a wall it could not scale.

AUTHOR UNKNOWN

Life is filled with stress, difficulty, and pressure. We cannot escape its influence. We seem to be attacked in family relationships, with physical illness, in accidents, and through natural disasters. Cell phones, beepers, e-mail, faxes, long lines, road rage, noise, jam-packed schedules, meetings, overcrowding, barking dogs, and children with temper tantrums can confront us on a daily basis. Stressed passengers freak out when their plane flight is delayed or canceled.

A certain amount of stress is good and healthy for us. An upcoming test will cause us to study more diligently. Downhill skiing will sharpen our focus and coordination. This type of stress will add fun, excitement, and productivity to our lives. However, undue stress can have a detrimental effect on us physically, emotionally, and spiritually. This type of stress creates anxiety and depression.

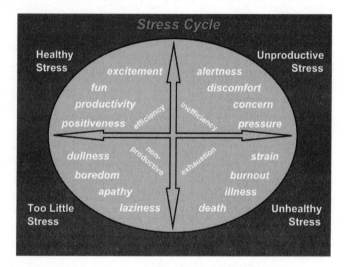

Stress has a residual quality to it. It builds up over time in our lives and leaks out in our bodies. Listed below are some of the warning signals of stress. See if you are experiencing any of them.

Emotional Signs of Stress	
boredom	irritability
confusion	listlessness
depression	nervousness
detachment	overexcitement

disorientation

escape thoughts

feeling low

forgetfulness

impatience

insecurity

paranoia

quick-temperedness

sadness

sleep loss

uneasiness

worry

Visceral Signs of Stress

cold chills

cold hands

colitis

cramps

diarrhea

dry mouth

fainting

heartburn

heart pounding

light-headedness

moist hands

nausea

sweating

ulcers

Musculoskeletal Signs of Stress

arthritis

back pain

cramps

fidgeting

fist clenching

grinding teeth

headaches

jaw tightening

shaky hands

stiff neck

stuttering

tense muscles

tics

twitches

Other Signs of Stress

cold sores

compulsiveness

exhaustion

fatigue

frequent colds

hair twisting

hay fever

heart disease

low spiritual life

low sex drive

nail biting

neglecting exercise

neglecting family

neglecting friends

neglecting fun

neglecting health

high alcohol use	neglecting rest
high caffeine use	no enthusiasm
high nicotine use	no vigor
high sugar use	obesity
jumpiness	obsessiveness

Following is the famous Holmes & Rahe Stress Test. It will give you some idea of how much stress you may be encountering at this time in your life. Take a moment to review it and add up your score. Your total will indicate your susceptibility to illness. This is a result of your body's resistance being low and because of the buildup of stress in your life for an extended period of time. Add points for each occurrence if there is more than one during the last 12 months.

HOLMES & RAHE STRESS TEST

Life Event	Occurrences	Stress Value	Your Score
death of a spouse		100	
divorce		73	
marital separation		65	
detention in jail		63	
death of close family member		63	
major personal injury or illness		53	
marriage difficulties		50	
being fired from work		47	
marital reconciliation		45	
retirement from work		47	
major change in health or behavior of family member		44	
pregnancy		40	
sexual difficulties		39	

Life Event	Occurrences	Stress Value	Your Score
gaining a new family member by birth, adoption, moving in		39	
major business readjustment, reorganization, bankruptcy		39	
major change in financial status— better or worse		38	
death of close friend		37	
changing to different line of work		36	
major change in arguments with spouse—more or less		35	
taking out a major mortgage or loan		31	
foreclosure on mortgage or loan		30	
major change in responsibilities at work—promotion or demotion		29	
son or daughter leaving home for marriage or school		29	
trouble with in-laws		29	
outstanding personal achievement		28	
spouse begins or ceases work		26	

Life Event	Occurrences	Stress Value	Your Score
beginning or ending school		26	
major change in living conditions		25	
revision of personal habits		24	
troubles with boss		23	
change in work hours or conditions		20	
change in residence		20	
changing to a new school		20	
change in recreation— more or less		19	
change in church activities		19	
change in social activities		18	
taking out a minor mortgage or loan		17	
change in sleeping habits		16	
change in family get-togethers		15	
change in eating habits		15	
vacation		13	
Christmas		12	
minor violations of the law		11	
your total stress level score			

Score of 0–149—healthy state of being with normal stress

Score of 150–199—37% chance of encountering illness in near future

Score of 200–299—50% chance of encountering illness in near future

Score of 300 or more—80% chance of encountering illness in near future

---

Times of stress and difficulty are seasons of opportunity when the seeds of progress are sown.

THOMAS F. WOODLOCK

❖ ❖ ❖

Most stress is caused by people who overestimate the importance of their problems.

MICHAEL LEBOEUF

4

The DISTORTED MIND
The Power of Negative Thoughts

❖ ❖ ❖

Our best friends and our worst enemies are our thoughts.
A thought can do us more good
than a doctor, a banker, or a faithful friend.
It can also do us more harm than a brick.

FRANK CRANE

AS YOU HAVE PROBABLY NOTICED, the emotional, visceral, musculo-
skeletal, and other signs of stress are similar to the signs for anxiety and
depression. The reason is that they are all closely related. They all deal
with relationships and events in life that cause distress in people. Anxiety
and depression are not causal; they are the result of something. Something
makes you anxious, and something makes you depressed. What is this
mysterious something? Is it a chemical imbalance in your body? Is it an
illness or a disease of some kind? Is it inherited, or do you create it yourself? Are you a victim of something from outside your body and mind
that is attacking you? Why do you feel anxiety and depression? Why do
you feel stressed? Why are you having difficulty going to sleep at night?
And why do you feel as if you are beginning to run down physically?

To better get a handle on the causes of anxiety and depression, we need
to take a look at our emotions. What triggers emotions in our lives? In her
book *Depression Is a Choice,* A.B. Curtiss shares some insightful words:

> If the three most important things in real estate are location,
> location, and location, then the three most important things

in mental health are perception, perception, and perception. It is our perception of depression that is the problem more than the low level of serotonin that seems to cause the trouble.

Anxiety and depression are triggered by past events in our lives or by what we think will happen in the future. Usually past and future events are both involved. As we look at a past event or a possible future event, we begin to form ideas about it. We affirm beliefs that could be rational or completely irrational. We also have assumptions that could be reasonable or unreasonable. These are tied to expectations that may be logical or illogical. This is further complicated by valid or invalid needs, fair or unfair demands, and good or bad attitudes. These are all enhanced by perceptions that may be accurate or inaccurate. This then becomes our version of reality. Our reality could be based on a good foundation or on a shaky foundation.

Our perception of the event may then give rise to "fight or flight" emotions. The "fight" emotion—anger—can lead to frustration, resentment, and depression. The "flight" emotion—fear—can lead to concern, worry, and anxiety. But if our perception leads to peaceful feelings, we relax and are thankful, accepting, and happy.

Another way to look at our emotions is to view them like dominos in a line. For example, let's say that we experience a relational event with someone who is close to us. He could say something or do something that hurts us deeply. Whether he was really trying to hurt us is not the issue at this point. In this case, perception is reality. If we perceive that he was trying to hurt us, we will experience corresponding negative emotions.

Because of that perception, we will feel disappointed. The disappointment can be compounded by anger (at what he did), fear (that the relationship may be damaged), or revenge (the desire to get even). If the problem is not solved, it can lead to frustration and defensive reactions, such as withdrawal (moving away from him), attack (trying to hurt him or put him down), or compromise (which doesn't really deal with the issue at hand and resolve it).

The turmoil we feel inside over the damaged relationship can give rise to anxiety and depression. As anxiety and depression begin to deepen, we begin to lose trust with the other person. *(How could he do this to me? It's not right!)* Soon after we lose trust, we also lose respect for the person. Before long, resentment, bitterness, and hatred take root.

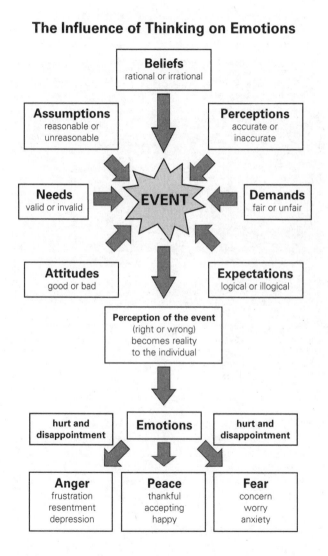

The Influence of Thinking on Emotions

Beliefs
rational or irrational

Assumptions
reasonable or
unreasonable

Perceptions
accurate or
inaccurate

Needs
valid or invalid

EVENT

Demands
fair or unfair

Attitudes
good or bad

Expectations
logical or illogical

Perception of the event
(right or wrong)
becomes reality
to the individual

hurt and
disappointment

Emotions

hurt and
disappointment

Anger
frustration
resentment
depression

Peace
thankful
accepting
happy

Fear
concern
worry
anxiety

This pattern can become a habitual response. The next time I am hurt, I will follow the same emotional route. Soon it becomes a well-worn path in my experience and other relationships.

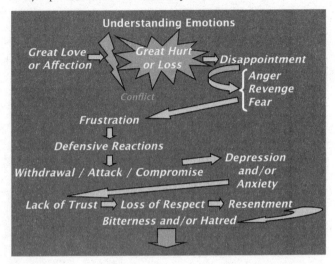

Because we want to avoid more anxiety and depression, we may begin using defense mechanisms to protect ourselves. We might start to withdraw from other people, creating our own safety zones of isolation. Or we may cover our emotional distress with humor. If we're always laughing and joking, we can fool people the same way Grimaldi the clown did. Or we can go the opposite direction and become angry people, attacking anyone who threatens us before he has a chance to hurt us.

We could choose to bounce in and out of friendships, in and out of jobs, and in and out of life. In that way we can enjoy relationships until we might get hurt again and then escape at the last moment. Staying in authentic, long-lasting relationships, which include both the good and the bad, may require more energy, commitment, and honesty than we are willing to muster. To cut and run is much easier.

Taking on the role of the martyr *(poor me—please feel sorry for me)* is another option. That way we become the center of attention and get lots of sympathy for the pain we suffer. And of course, some people turn to drugs or alcohol to mask their hurts, angers, and fears, settling for temporary relief but in reality only making their problems worse.

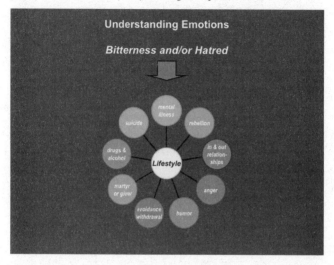

In this context, we also see that a mental illness can be a defense mechanism that protects us from experiencing more pain. *My illness is making me behave this way,* we think, and so we excuse ourselves from taking responsibility for our thoughts, actions, and behavior. And if that doesn't solve the problem, some people turn to suicide rather than facing their problems and working to find more helpful solutions.

If A.B. Curtiss is correct in saying that the key to mental health is perception, perception, perception (and I think she is), how do we gain control of our perceptions? How can we change our views of specific circumstances and events, personal relationships, and life in general? How do I learn to replace the negative and unwanted emotions, moods, and feelings with the positive? How do I overcome anxiety and depression?

We start with a reeducation of where our feelings, moods, and emotions come from. They are responses to the thoughts we choose to entertain.

Our mind gives direction to the thinking process. We can think positive thoughts, or we can think negative thoughts. Our will gives us the power or energy to change our minds and choose the right track or the wrong track. Our emotions follow wherever the engine leads them like cars on a train. Emotions can be very strong and influential, but they always follow the mind's direction.

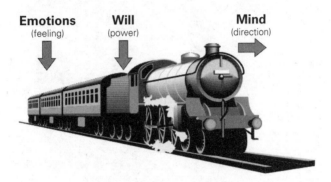

Emotions (feeling)   **Will** (power)   **Mind** (direction)

For example, let's say you have been encountering very difficult financial responsibilities. You haven't been fired, but you had an automobile accident and the repairs cost more than you expected. Your son broke his arm in soccer practice, and your insurance didn't cover all the expenses. Your parents had to move from their home, and you had to assist them. Along with these pressures are the bills left from Christmas and some of your daughter's college education expenses.

Viewing Problems in Degrees

Worry   Anxiety

Concern   Phobias

Fears

These financial pressures begin to create concerns than can turn into worries. As time moves forward and no relief is in sight, you find yourself becoming anxious and irritated. Your anxiety about paying bills makes you obsessive about everyone in your family turning off the lights and turning down the heat. You become compulsive about picking up every plastic bottle and every can lying on the ground so you can cash them in to help pay your bills. You even go next door and get all of your neighbor's cans and bottles.

Before long your whole financial situation begins to overwhelm you. Depression begins to settle in. You have trouble sleeping at night. You don't see any way out. Your energy level begins to drop, and you wish the merry-go-round of life would stop so you could get off.

What is happening? Do you have a psychological disease? A mental illness? Has the serotonin in your brain malfunctioned, causing you to feel the way you do? Has a chemical imbalance caused your anxiety and depression to increase? Would taking some drug help with the emotional turmoil you are feeling? Of course not. You've simply allowed your mind to focus on the negative and lead you into depression.

One day while you're in the middle of your deep depression, the doorbell rings. You open the door, and your mouth drops open in surprise. A group of people are standing outside yelling and holding signs. Television cameras are focused on you. You're trying to process what is happening when someone pushes a microphone into your face and says, "Congratulations! You just won the Publisher's Clearing House Sweepstakes!"

Now how do you feel? What happened to your emotions of anxiety and depression? Whammo! Did your serotonin level suddenly and automatically adjust itself, causing you to feel great? Did the drugs you were taking instantly cure your depression? Did your mental illness evaporate mysteriously? Why do you all of a sudden feel happy and begin to jump for joy? Quite simply, your perception of life has just changed. One second you are poor and unhappy and the next second you are rich and on top of the world.

How we wish changing our emotions was that simple. I'm here to tell you it *is* that simple…it's just not *easy*. If you are going to wait until your feelings change before you change your thinking, you're in for a long wait.

The great apostle Paul talked about this subject in his letter to the Philippians. He comments on changing our thinking and attitude by what we focus our thinking on.

GOD'S SECRET FORMULA FOR
CHANGING YOUR ATTITUDE

Philippians 4:4-9

Command:	Always be full of joy in the Lord; I say it again, rejoice!
Command:	Let everyone see that you are unselfish and considerate in all you do.
Motivation:	Remember that the Lord is coming soon.
Command:	Don't worry about anything; instead, pray about everything; tell God your needs, and don't forget to thank him for his answers.
Promise:	If you do this, you will experience God's peace, which is far more wonderful than the human mind can understand. His peace will keep your thoughts and your hearts quiet and at rest as you trust in Christ Jesus.
Closing:	And now, brothers, as I close this letter, let me say this one more thing:
Command:	Fix your thoughts on what is true and good and right.
Command:	Think about the things that are pure and lovely, and dwell on the fine, good things in others.
Command:	Think about all you can praise God for and be glad about.
Command:	Keep putting into practice all you learned from me and saw me doing,
Promise:	and the God of peace will be with you.

Paul is suggesting that peace comes when we stop thinking negative thoughts and choose to think positive thoughts. Wise King Solomon also touched on the importance of the thinking process when he said, "When a man is gloomy, everything seems to go wrong; when he is cheerful, everything seems right!"(Proverbs 15:15).

Every event that a man would master must be mounted on the run, and no man ever caught the reins of thought except as it galloped past him.

OLIVER WENDELL HOLMES

5

The DISCOVERING MIND
Accepting Responsibility

❖ ❖ ❖

Men occasionally stumble over the truth,
but most of them pick themselves up and hurry off as if
nothing had happened.

WINSTON CHURCHILL

FEW PEOPLE WHO LIVED IN CALIFORNIA in the '70s will forget the classic case of Dan White. His political dreams were dashed when San Francisco mayor George Moscone and supervisor Harvey Milk refused to reappoint White as a supervisor. White gained entrance to city hall with a well-hidden gun and the intent to kill the man who destroyed his career. He climbed in through a window to avoid metal detectors, found the mayor's office, and shot him five times. He then reloaded, sought out Harvey Milk, and shot him four times.

At Dan White's trial, his lawyers went for the insanity plea. Psychiatrists insisted that White was suffering from diminished capacity, caused by living at home and consuming Cokes, Twinkies, and other junk food. This became known as the Twinkie Defense—White was not responsible for his actions; he was mentally ill. The Twinkies made him do it.

When John W. Hinckley Jr. shot President Ronald Reagan, Harvard psychiatrist Thomas Gutheil suggested that Hinckley was a victim suffering from a disease known as *erotomania,* in which a person believes that a celebrity is in love with him. Hinckley supposedly believed that actress Jodie Foster secretly loved him and that if he shot President Reagan,

Foster would reveal her affections. Therefore, Hinckley was supposedly not a terrorist or murderer. Rather, he was ill.

What If Mental Illness Doesn't Exist?

Mental illness is not an illness in the traditional medical sense. "Mental illness" is simply a metaphor to describe behaviors in a person's life. When we say that someone is lovesick, does he or she really have a physical disease? Of course not. When someone is homesick, is this a result of a virus or an infection? That would be ridiculous. "Homesick" is just a metaphor to describe a feeling. It is not a true illness. We often use this type of language for describing troubled relationships between people. The

---

PSYCHIATRIC HOTLINE

Welcome to the psychiatric hotline.

If you are obsessive-compulsive, please press 1 repeatedly.

If you are codependent, please ask someone to press 2 for you.

If you have panic disorder, please press 3. This indicates the number of minutes before someone will break into your home and kidnap you.

If you have multiple personalities, please press 4, 5, and 7.

If you are bipolar, please press 6 and 9. They seem to be opposite.

If you are anxious, think about all of the things that could go wrong if someone were to answer the phone.

If you are schizophrenic, listen carefully, and a small, quiet voice will tell you which number to press.

If you are a depressive, it doesn't matter which number you press. No one will answer.

If you have paranoid delusions, we know who you are and what you want. Just stay on the line so we can trace the call.

Thank you for calling the psychiatric hotline.

phrase "You make me sick" is not describing a disease. "He is a real pain in the neck" is not a diagnosis of a physical ailment. It may be descriptive of a damaged relationship, but it certainly is not a sickness or injury. Countless expressions describe feelings and behavior but have nothing to do with medical problems.

> Though this be madness, yet there is method in it.
>
> WILLIAM SHAKESPEARE

"Hard-hearted" does not mean that the heart turns to stone.

"Brokenhearted" does not mean the heart is cracked.

"Chickenhearted" does not mean someone has received a transplant.

"She turns my stomach" does not mean that someone flips you over.

"You're a pain in the rear" does not mean that someone has kicked you.

"I feel weighted down" does not mean a steamroller has crushed you.

"He makes me throw up" does not mean someone jams their fingers down your throat.

But if mental illness doesn't exist, are troubled people well? The answer is yes, they are well medically. However, they're not feeling good emotionally. They are unhappy. People can be well in the physical and medical sense and still be unhappy in the emotional sense.

Psychobabble

Herein lies the problem. Prevailing medical and psychological models treat some moods like anxiety and depression as illnesses. Some people have expanded this even further by saying crime is an illness. Poverty is an illness. Overeating is an illness (bulimia). Undereating is an illness (anorexia nervosa). Overdrinking is an illness (alcoholism). Betting too much money is an illness (pathological gambling). Stealing things from stores is an illness (kleptomania). The fear of being in public places is an illness (agoraphobia).

Not paying attention is an illness (attention deficit disorder with hyperactivity). Setting a building on fire is an illness (pyromania). A man dressing in women's clothes has an illness (transvestism). Selfish pride

> Schizophrenia is the name for a condition that most psychiatrists ascribe to patients they call schizophrenic.
>
> R.D. LAING

is an illness (narcissistic personality disorder). Smoking too much is an illness (tobacco use disorder). Having persistent thoughts and repetitive behaviors is an illness (obsessive-compulsive disorder). Having a hurtful past experience is an illness (post-traumatic stress disorder).

Who Is Responsible?

This foolishness needs to stop. How long should we go on describing socially unacceptable behaviors as illnesses? Are we helping people when we tell them they are sick when they are simply exercising behaviors that irritate themselves and annoy other people?

This does not in any way mean that problems do not exist. Life is filled with personal misery. Social unrest has been part of the human condition since recorded history began. Everyone has experienced suffering at some time in his or her life. So what else is new? Although these experiences are common regardless of race or ethnic origin, they aren't diseases. They are not illnesses. When we call unpleasantness, suffering, pain, or criminal behavior a disease, we rob ourselves of integrity and honesty. When we categorize hurtful individual actions as illnesses, we undermine individual responsibility and accountability. When we take away responsibility and accountability, we destroy hope of change.

To call wickedness or strange behavior an illness creates an excuse for the behavior to continue. "I'm not responsible; my illness makes me act this way." "If only the disease would go away, I wouldn't act the way I do." "If I didn't have this illness, I wouldn't be the failure I am." Blame shifting has become a way of life for many people.

A Rose Garden?

If I accept responsibility for my actions, will my life become a rose garden? Will I be happy all the time? Will everything run smoothly for me? Will I escape the problems that other people face? Of course not.

We have no guarantee that life will be one big, joyous party. All of human history and personal experience argue against that type of thinking.

The struggles of life make us strong and mature. We admire those who have endured tough times and have emerged victorious. We desire to have the strength of character these people display. The only problem is that we want to gain this fortitude without the pain. We want the positive character traits without going through the fire of adversity.

Once I do away with the myth of mental illness, I immediately gain hope. I am responsible for most of the predicaments in which I find myself. I play a part in the process. Once I realize this, I can get on with the business of making positive changes

> This tendency to avoid problems and the emotional suffering inherent in them is the primary basis of all human mental illness.
>
> M. SCOTT PECK

in my life. I can learn how to face problems and difficulties. I can become the veteran of life who faces struggles with courage and a positive spirit.

Diseases of the Brain

Diseases of the brain do exist, such as cerebral syphilis, encephalitis, frontal lobe and temporal lobe tumors, cerebral arteriosclerosis and strokes and embolisms, aphasia and apraxia, senile dementia, and Alzheimer's disease. These are true illnesses. Also, some chemical imbalances in the human body directly influence the emotions and the thinking process. Diabetes, hypoglycemia, thyroid imbalances, and estrogen deficiencies are a few causes of these imbalances. Birth defects, mental retardation, and accidents also affect the brain and the thinking process. All of the above are true diseases, illnesses, or physical defects. They are understandable and can be traced to their origin. They are diseases of the body and brain…but they are not mental illness.

No microorganism enters my body, moves to the brain, and causes me to murder my spouse. I may be drunk, jealous, or enraged, but I'm not ill.

No parasite comes from the outside and causes me to become a chronic liar or thief. These are chosen human behaviors that have nothing to do with disease.

Bacteria does not cause me to overeat or starve myself. A broken relationship or a low self-image may be the cause, but not some type of germ.

Viruses do not cause me to drink, use drugs, gamble, or take off my clothes in public places. These are behaviors of choice, not random illnesses that overtake my body.

> Neurotics build castles in the air. Psychotics live in the castles. Psychiatrists collect the rent.

How do we deal with so-called mental illness today? How do we cure diseases of mental dysfunction? The most common approaches utilize drugs, electric shock, surgery, therapy sessions…or we commit people to mental hospitals.

Drugs are good for infections and true sickness, but drugs do not cure a negative thinking process. Taking drugs only numbs, slows, and dulls thinking. And when someone stops taking drugs, all of the difficulties of life are still there.

Drugs do not eliminate stress, improve your self-image, or heal broken relationships. They do not teach you life-coping skills or take away hurt and loss from your life.

Anxiety and depression are not diseases. They are not illnesses. They are thinking processes. Drugs can influence a thinking process, but they don't change it. We will talk about changing your thinking later in the book.

We acknowledge certain brain diseases, birth defects, and chemical imbalances. But these medical conditions do not affect the general population on a large scale. They affect a very small minority of people. About 5 percent of those with mental health issues also have chemical or physical issues. The vast majority of people who encounter depression, anxiety, and other problems and difficulties are not ill medically. They are troubled and not feeling good emotionally, but they are not diseased or sick.

Most problems that are classified as some form of mental illness are in reality caused by…

- broken and conflicted relationships
- unspoken, unfulfilled, or unrealistic expectations of life
- guilt over not doing what we should do
- disobedience
- lack of exercise
- poor diet or overeating
- too much television

- not accepting responsibility
- prolonged sleep loss
- faulty reasoning
- emptiness and loneliness
- lack of meaning and purpose
- alienation and separation
- buildup of various stressful events
- death of a loved one
- inability to adjust to and accept hurtful experiences
- unwillingness to let go of the past and forgive others
- low self-image or high perfectionistic standards

We must also stop calling extreme wickedness mental illness. We must put an end to telling people they are sick when the truth is that they are just exercising behaviors with which they are not happy and that others get upset over. We need to realize that we may be holding unrealistic expectations about life and relationships with people.

It is not healthy for individuals or society in general to believe that they are victims with no control over their lives or behavior. This type of advice robs the individual of integrity and self-respect. It creates a patient-and-doctor relationship. It encourages dependency and introversion.

Mental, emotional, and spiritual growth come from facing problems rather than running from them. Growth involves struggle, pain, and courage. It requires the exercise of the will and the determination not to give up. Our spirit and character are molded out of the battles and conflicts of life. When we accept responsibility for our own actions and attitudes, we grow toward maturity. We then gain self-respect and begin to adjust to the pain that is common to all people. As a result we become healthier because of our ownership.

> Dear brothers, is your life full of difficulties and temptations? Then be happy, for when the way is rough, your patience has a chance to grow. So let it grow, and don't try to squirm out of your problems. For when your patience is finally in full bloom, then you will be ready for anything, strong in character, full and complete.
>
> JAMES 1:2-4

6

The DISCERNING MIND
Another Way to View Mental Illness

❖ ❖ ❖

*After a spirit of discernment, the next rarest
things in the world are diamonds and pearls.*

JEAN DE LA BRUYÈRE

MARK TWAIN ONCE REMARKED, "One of the striking differences
between a cat and a lie is that the cat only has nine lives." Someone else
has said, "Repeat a lie long enough, and it will be believed as truth."

Harriet Beecher Stowe was the mother of seven children and the sister
of the renowned clergyman Henry Ward Beecher and the reformer and
educator Catharine Beecher. Harriet Beecher Stowe will always be remem-
bered as the author of the famous antislavery book *Uncle Tom's Cabin*.
She made an interesting comment: "Half the misery in the world comes
of want of courage to speak and to hear the truth plainly, and in a spirit
of love."

Those who struggle with anxiety and depression experience a great
deal of misery. Without question, millions are suffering more than they
should. Where are all these people going to get help and relief? Does the
only answer lie in pharmacology? Or could there possibly be some other
way?

Be wary of uncritically believing that the anxiety and depression you
are experiencing are caused by a chemical imbalance in your brain, and
that you can cure your chemical imbalance by taking drugs. Chemical
imbalances do exist in some people who are encountering depression and

various mental struggles. However, no proof exists at all that this small imbalance is the cause of any mental disorder. On the contrary, the more rational explanation is that a chemical imbalance is the *result* of emotional turmoil, not the *cause*. And drugs may temporarily mask, blur, or deaden emotions, but they do not resolve or correct mental issues in a person's life. In later chapters we will examine how to specifically deal with anxiety and depression.

Question #1: Which came first, the chicken or the egg?

Answer: The chicken came first. God doesn't lay any eggs.

Question #2: Which comes first, chemical responses or emotions?

Answer: Thinking comes first, and that gives rise to emotions.

Thinking and emotions are combinations of electrical and chemical reactions in the body. Changes in the chemical process in the body are primarily results of thoughts and perceptions. Chemical changes in the body can also be influenced by illness, accidents, injury, food, drugs, alcohol, and other environmental factors. In other words, something causes the chemical change. The question remains, what is the cause? This is the million-dollar question.

A person would not be likely to be enjoying a healthy and happy life…and then one day, slam bam, experience a chemical change without a causal factor. Healthiness and happiness would suddenly change to fear, anger, worry, anxiety, depression, phobia, paranoia, bipolar behavior, or thoughts of suicide. It simply does not happen that way.

Chemical changes in the body are real, of course. But they are not the initial causes of an unhealthy lifestyle, negative and disruptive thoughts, devastating emotions, bizarre behavior, or criminal acts. The chemical changes are results of these things. Once we acknowledge this, we have hope for change. Otherwise, we are the hapless victims of fate without any volitional participation in life. The plain fact is that you are a player in life.

For several reasons, what I have suggested is not always readily received. One reason is ignorance. Very few people examine evidence and claims on their own. They simply trust medical professionals or those who seem to know more than they do. They do not have the interest or take the time to seek knowledge themselves. Another reason to not challenge the medical model of chemical imbalance is that if I do, I can no longer blame my emotions and behavior on someone or something else over which I have no control. I have to take responsibility for my thoughts, emotions, and behaviors. This requires too much honesty, energy, and time. It is too messy, and maturing and growing up as an adult is not always fun. I don't want to acknowledge that life has a lot of difficulties to it. Wallowing in my misery, cultivating my fears, and growing my angers are all much easier. Dealing with conflict and damaged relationships can be too painful. A third reason the challenge to chemical imbalance is not readily received comes from those who produce the drugs.

Dr. Joseph Glenmullen, in his book *Prozac Backlash,* cites several cases where questionable practices occurred with regard to drug research. The first involved a controversy over the drug Prozac. Some people on the drug were experiencing intense, violent, suicidal thoughts as a result of taking the medication. Dr. Gary Tollefson wrote an article for the *American Journal of Psychiatry* defending Prozac. He suggested that "we should not lose sight of its beneficial addition to our therapeutic armamentarium." He went on to suggest that it was "potentially counterproductive" to talk about the negative side effects of the drug. Tollefson neglected to identify the fact that he was an employee of Eli Lilly, the pharmaceutical company that introduced Prozac.[1]

The early part of the 1990s saw such an outcry about the side effects of Prozac that the FDA put together a panel of experts to help determine how the drug should be handled. Dr. Glenmullen gives us insight about the panel.

> Who were the blue-ribbon, independent experts on the Prozac panel? There were nine doctors, five of whose financial ties to the pharmaceutical industry—including the manufacturers of serotonin boosters—required the FDA to "waive" its own standards regarding conflicts of interest. In addition, six consultants were appointed to advise the panel. Four of the six consultants required conflict-of-interest waivers.[2]

> One of the most highly publicized scandals surfaced in the spring of 1997. The chairman of the department of psychiatry at the Medical College of Georgia, psychopharmacologist Richard Borison, and another professor in his department, Bruce Diamond, were indicted by the Georgia Attorney General on 172 counts of bribery, racketeering, forgeries, and endangering patients in connection with clinical testing of psychiatric medications for some twenty pharmaceutical

companies over a decade. During this time, the two professors published more than twenty articles in scholarly journals and built national reputations based on their "research" on depression, anxiety, schizophrenia, and Alzheimer's disease. The April 1997 *Psychiatric Times* reported that one "bribery count in the indictment alleges that Borison and Diamond paid an undisclosed sum to an MCG [Medical College of Georgia] employee in exchange for her not filing a complaint regarding a patient suicide that occurred during a clinical study." From 1989 to 1996 alone, these two psychopharmacologists made more than $10 million on drug research, a rare glimpse into the profitability of testing psychiatric drugs.[3]

A.B. Curtiss offers similar findings in *Depression Is a Choice:*

> Dr. Sheldon Krimsky of Tufts University has reported that in an investigation of 800 scientific papers he made in 1997, 34 percent of the authors had conflicts of interest with financial ties that were not disclosed. Of 210 scientific journals surveyed, all of them had such funding, and only 25 percent revealed it. A 1998 study showed that "virtually every researcher publicly supporting the use of new hypersensitive drugs had financial ties to drug manufacturers."[4]

This does not mean that every researcher is unethical or doing something illegal. It does, however, point to the fact that the various drug companies have a vital interest in the growth of the drug industry. This also does not suggest that the drug companies are not trying to develop medicines that help people. But if you think their motives are simply to help people and that the amount of money they make is not a factor, you may not be facing reality.

Have you seen any TV advertisements for drugs? How much do you think commercial advertising is costing the drug companies? Why do you think they continue to advertise? Drug companies make billions of dollars each year. They have a very large stake in keeping the medical model of mental illness alive.

There are two strong models in the battle for mental health: the medical model and the counseling model. One is based on the premise that a mental illness exists. The second approach suggests that people experience mental disorder and maladaptation but not a mental disease. I believe that one model leads to dependency and discouragement while the other model leads to responsibility and hope. I want to help you move from the medical model to the counseling model of dealing with anxiety and depression.

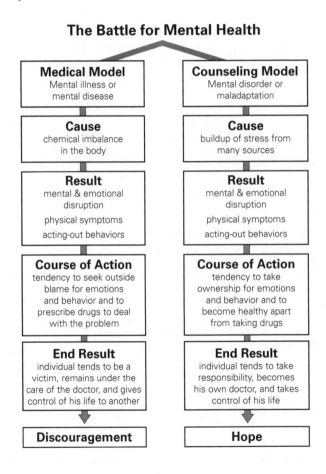

The Battle for Mental Health

Medical Model	Counseling Model
Mental illness or mental disease	Mental disorder or maladaptation
Cause chemical imbalance in the body	**Cause** buildup of stress from many sources
Result mental & emotional disruption physical symptoms acting-out behaviors	**Result** mental & emotional disruption physical symptoms acting-out behaviors
Course of Action tendency to seek outside blame for emotions and behavior and to prescribe drugs to deal with the problem	**Course of Action** tendency to take ownership for emotions and behavior and to become healthy apart from taking drugs
End Result individual tends to be a victim, remains under the care of the doctor, and gives control of his life to another	**End Result** individual tends to take responsibility, becomes his own doctor, and takes control of his life
Discouragement	**Hope**

To understand the counseling model, we must clarify what an illness is. Illnesses spring from several different causes. We can have what is called a congenital illness. This is something that is inherited from our parents or grandparents. The prevalence of heart disease in some families is an example of this.

Another way we could contract an illness is through a virus. A virus is a microorganism or tiny germ. A virus is smaller than a bacterium and is an incomplete organism. It must live like a parasite on larger living cells. It penetrates the host cell and forms more virus particles. Doctors believe that viruses transmit more than 50 diseases. Drugs that seem to curb bacteria have no effect on viruses. The treatment for viruses is to make the patient as comfortable as possible to prevent complications.

Bacteria are simple one-celled organisms. They are the most numerous of all organisms and are found almost everywhere. Some researchers estimate that a cubic foot of air contains more than 100 bacteria. The four basic types of bacteria are cocci, vibrios, bacilli, and spirilla. Helpful bacteria break down animal flesh and plants after they die. Bacteria are used to make buttermilk, cheese, vinegar, sauerkraut, and silage. Bacteria are also used in sewage treatment plants to help purify water. Harmful bacteria include things like anthrax, diphtheria, gonorrhea, leprosy, pneumonia, tetanus, tuberculosis, typhoid fever, and whooping cough.

There are about 20,000 different kinds of protozoa, the lowest form of life in the animal kingdom. The four major types of protozoa are flagellates, amoeboids, sporozoans, and ciliates. They reproduce by splitting in two. Protozoas are responsible for illnesses such as giardia, malaria, and African sleeping sickness.

Fungi are simple plants. Scientists have identified about 75,000 species or kinds of fungi. Parasitic fungi live on plants and animals and can be harmful in the form of smuts, rusts, and mildew. Other parasitic fungi can cause illness in people.

Chemical imbalances can also cause physical illness. Diabetes, hypoglycemia, thyroid imbalance, and estrogen deficiencies are a few problems chemical imbalances can cause.

Just growing old can bring upon illness as body organs begin to malfunction and deteriorate. The elderly unfortunately become familiar with strokes, senile dementia, and Alzheimer's disease.

And various environmental factors can bring about such physical ailments as hearing loss, poisoning, lung and breathing problems, and skin cancer.

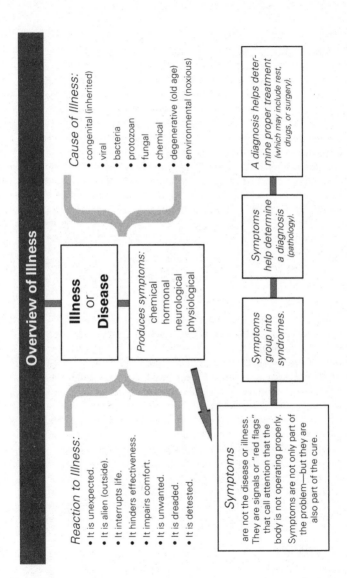

Overview of Illness

Illness
or
Disease

Cause of Illness:
- congenital (inherited)
- viral
- bacteria
- protozoan
- fungal
- chemical
- degenerative (old age)
- environmental (noxious)

Produces symptoms:
chemical
hormonal
neurological
physiological

Reaction to Illness:
- It is unexpected.
- It is alien (outside).
- It interrupts life.
- It hinders effectiveness.
- It impairs comfort.
- It is unwanted.
- It is dreaded.
- It is detested.

Symptoms

are not the disease or illness. They are signals or "red flags" that call attention that the body is not operating properly. Symptoms are not only part of the problem—but they are also part of the cure.

Symptoms group into syndromes.

Symptoms help determine a diagnosis (pathology).

A diagnosis helps determine proper treatment (which may include rest, drugs, or surgery).

Illness is usually unexpected. It often seems to come from outside the body. It interrupts our life and hinders our effectiveness.

The reaction in a human body to illness is very predictable. As illness enters a body, the body develops symptoms. These symptoms call attention to the fact that the body is not operating properly. A doctor looks for symptoms to provide a clue to the nature of the illness. Most diseases have symptoms that are common to all people regardless of their culture or background. A group of symptoms create a syndrome. A diagnosis of symptoms gives the doctor some idea where the illness came from and where it will most likely lead. The symptoms not only tell the nature of the illness but direct the doctor in the treatment, which can include rest, drugs, and surgery.

> Physicians think they do a lot for a patient when they give his disease a name.
>
> IMMANUEL KANT

Diseases are often divided into three categories. The first is organic disease. This is anything that adversely affects the cellular structure and smooth operation of the body. Organic diseases can be infectious or noninfectious. Infectious diseases can be transmitted by microorganisms, viruses, bacteria, parasites, and fungi. They damage the body by releasing poisons or toxins and/or by reproduction, as with the common cold or bird flu.

Noninfectious diseases are not communicable. They are degenerative processes brought about by heredity, birth defects, nutritional habits, a noxious environment, or old age. They include things like heart disease, arthritis, and kidney failure.

Both infectious and noninfectious diseases can be acute (short and severe) or chronic (persisting). Both can slow a person down and result in death. This, of course, is a very quick overview.

The second category of disease is conversion reactions. In a conversion reaction, the body loses some of its functions without structural impairment. No organ destruction causes the impairment. The individual experiences physical disabilities that help the body cope with unbearable stress. Some people experience temporary blindness, deafness, the inability to speak, or the paralysis of a limb. Some researchers have called conversion reactions a form of hysteria.

The third category of disease is psychosomatic disease. This is a

Understanding Disease

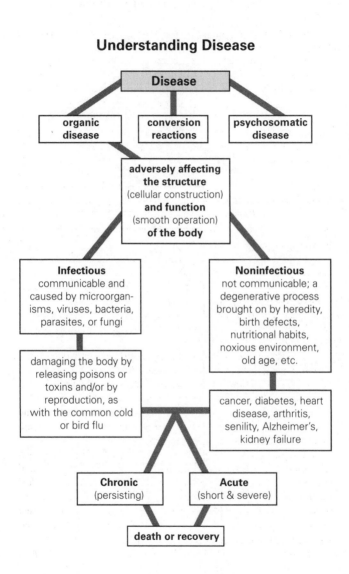

Understanding Disease

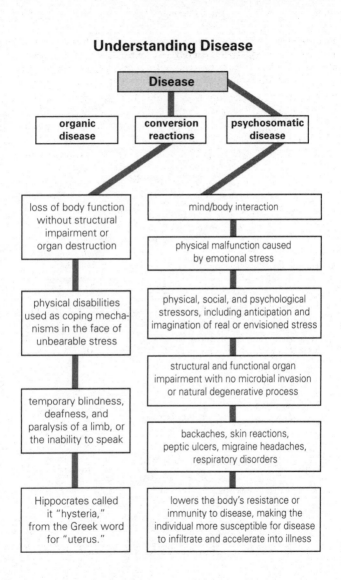

malfunction of the body caused by emotional stress. It involves an anticipation of real or envisioned stress or problems. No microbial invasion causes the structural and functional organ impairment. No degenerative process takes place in the organs. Yet the sufferers will have backaches, skin reactions, peptic ulcers, respiratory disorders, or migraine headaches. They can have problems with diarrhea and constipation and upset stomach. In this state the individuals' resistance and immunity to disease are lowered. They can be susceptible to other diseases.

We are hard-pressed to prove that "mental illness" is congenital, or inherited. The American Psychological Association suggests that people who come from homes in which one of the family members is anxious or depressed are up to three times more likely to experience anxiety and depression than those who come from healthy homes.

Hello! Of course they would. Anxious and depressed individuals are hard to live with. Just trying to cope with their moods makes you anxious and depressed. That does not, however, mean that you inherited anxiety and depression. We don't inherit someone else's emotions, moods, or behaviors. Other people's moods can affect our thinking and well-being, but they are not inherited.

Mental problems are sometimes difficult to deal with. Without question, emotions can be very painful to live with. Feelings can affect how our body functions. We've all had that experience. But as difficult as all of this is, emotional distress is not a disease or illness in the true medical sense.

7

The DISCRIMINATING MIND
Chemical Imbalance

❖ ❖ ❖

One out of four people in this country is mentally imbalanced. Think of your three closest friends. If they seem okay, then you're the one.

ANN LANDERS

WHAT ABOUT THE INSANE? What about all of the crazy people? Don't they have a mental illness? Mark Twain commented, "When we remember we are all mad, the mysteries disappear and life stands explained."

Human history has always witnessed people who have been called crazy, individuals who didn't march to the same drummer as everyone else. Some of these people harmed other people, and some harmed themselves. Most were just very different from the average person and didn't hurt anyone. Society has always had a difficult time dealing with these people.

Down through the years, philosophers, artists, clergymen, scientists, and physicians have endeavored to understand the nature of man. They have tried to understand his persistent fears and the motivation for his behavior. Their approaches have basically fallen into three categories:

1. They have looked for external organic and physical causes for abnormal behavior. This has involved the biological and medical sciences.

2. They have attempted to discover internal psychological reasons for people's thoughts and actions. This has given

rise to psychological studies and countless theories as to the motivation of human beings.

3. They have considered the influence of the stars, demons, magic, or the gods on human behavior. This viewpoint has resulted in fears, superstition, magical rituals, exorcism, incantations, intimidation, forced confessions, torture, and death.

The Babylonians and Egyptians practiced astrology and believed that the stars influenced human behavior. They used magical procedures to deal with strange conduct.

The Greeks believed that insanity came from the gods. They also believed that the four body humors—blood, phlegm, yellow bile, and black bile—determined how people acted. They thought that hysteria was caused by a wandering uterus, loosened from its moorings in the pelvic cavity. They also believed that only marriage and intercourse could cure the condition.

The Arabs saw the insane as divinely inspired and not victims of demons. They built a number of asylums for the people they believed were mentally sick.

In the 1300s and 1400s, witch hunts arose in Europe. An antierotic movement began. Witches (mostly women) were blamed for men's licentiousness. The general population thought witches could change men into animals by use of magical arts. People also believed that witches could keep women from having children and could produce abortions. Diseases came from witchcraft, and plagues were the result of sins. People were burned at the stake for their socially unacceptable behavior.

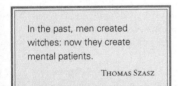

In the past, men created witches: now they create mental patients.

THOMAS SZASZ

In 1547, the Bethlem Royal Hospital was founded in London, England. It was later transformed into a mental hospital. The name "Bethlem" was mispronounced by many people as "Bedlam." The hospital soon became a curiosity for those in society. Visitors would come to watch the patients rage, scream, and babble incoherently. The inmates at "Bedlam" laughed strangely, tore their clothing, and excreted anywhere. At the height of its operation, "Bedlam" entertained more than 96,000 visitors a year. It became a human zoo, a psychological theme park.

During the 1700s and 1800s, asylums housed the insane, deformed, mentally retarded, and destitutes. Often the asylums or "madhouses" would have as many as 500 patients at a time. The "lunatics" were confined in iron cages with chains and manacles. Rape and murder were commonplace in the asylums. Often records were forged to hide details of embezzlement of funds, unexplained deaths, and records of *normal* individuals forced into the asylums by relatives.

The "crazy" were exposed to utter filth and neglect. Sicknesses were left untreated. Often the inmates were chained to walls and left naked. Some lost toes due to frostbite. Beatings, whippings, restraint in wooden cribs, and other forms of maltreatment occurred frequently. The food was infested with maggots and insects.

Asylum staff would bleed patients to drain off the mental illness. They also used electric shock, drugs, and surgery. They wrapped patients in cold sheets, causing the prisoners to scream for hours. They threw ice-cold water on the patients, whose muscles and joints would atrophy due to restraints and the lack of exercise.

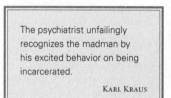

The psychiatrist unfailingly recognizes the madman by his excited behavior on being incarcerated.

KARL KRAUS

A "spinning chair" was invented to calm those who were out of control. Doctors believed that congested blood in the brain led to mental illness, and they thought this condition would be relieved by rotary motion. The spinning chair caused the patients to become disoriented, vomit, and finally pass out.

In the mid-1800s, reformers tried to change the conditions of the asylums. Individuals like Philippe Pinel, William Battie, John Conolly, Benjamin Rush, Thomas Kirkbride, Dorothea L. Dix, and William James deplored the treatment given at state hospitals. They believed benevolence and kindness were better cures. They strove to change the image of the "insane and mad." Over the years, their impact and that of others has helped to change the brutality and harshness of asylums. Their influence caused a host of people to take a serious look at those who were suffering because of emotional problems. Many learned individuals began to spend their lives in search of answers for the human condition.

Do we still have people today that seem to be crazy? Do doctors have difficulty dealing with or changing their behavior? The answer is yes. Man has not yet answered all of the questions surrounding mental dysfunction. A great deal of mystery plagues what the medical model calls a disease or illness and the counseling model calls mental dysfunction or maladaptation. The medical model looks for a cause in chemical imbalance while the counseling model focuses on dealing with stress.

Many questions about mental health remain unanswered. But that is no reason to label it as an illness, and help and encouragement are available for the average person who is encountering anxiety or depression.

What's All This Talk Concerning Serotonin About?

The human brain weighs about three pounds. That's only about 2 percent of the body's weight, but it consumes 20 percent of the body's energy. An estimated 1,000,000,000,000,000 nerve cells in the brain are connected by electrical pathways that impulses travel. These nerve cells include a nucleus in the cell body and axon roadways, which connect with dendrite docking stations. Where the axons and dendrites meet, chemical reactions take place. Neurotransmitters carry these chemical reactions across the synaptic gap between the sending and receiving cells. Messages can move both directions.

Scientists believe more than a hundred kinds of neurotransmitters exist, but only a little over thirty have been identified. Three of these 30 neurotransmitters seem to have some relationship with depression. They are epinephrine, serotonin, and dopamine. They wander through the pleasure centers of the brain—the hypothalamus and the limbic system. They influence our emotions, appetite, sleep, sexuality, fear, memory, and reaction to stress.

Some severely depressed individuals have a lowered serotonin level. This drop has caused researchers to suggest that the lack of serotonin caused the depression. This suggestion has taken off like a runaway freight train. But the question still remains unanswered: Does a drop in serotonin actually cause depression?

Let me lay a little bit of a foundation. As you read any studies about this subject, use your critical thinking skills. The reports are full of words that are often misleading.

"Serotonin *could* influence…"

"Serotonin *might* play a part…"

"Studies *seem* to indicate…"

"Doctors *suggest* a link to serotonin…"

"There *may be* a strong tie to low levels of serotonin…"

"Serotonin is *probably* involved with…"

"It *appears* that serotonin…"

"The link between low levels of serotonin and depressive illness is *unclear*…"

Or my favorite: "Low levels of serotonin *clearly seem* to trigger mood disorders."

How do researchers measure serotonin? It is impossible to cut into someone's brain, separate an individual synaptic gap out of the millions of synaptic gaps, and monitor the chemical reaction as a person either moves into depression or out of depression. It simply cannot be done.

The chemical reactions that take place in the synaptic gap could be likened to the firing of a spark plug in an internal combustion engine. The electrical spark sets off an explosion that forces the piston to move. Similarly, a chemical reaction (like the spark plug explosion) takes place in the brain as messages pass from the axon to the dendrite. Eventually, this reaction produces some kind of motion or thought in the person. We cannot yet measure this process.

How are we going to test for serotonin? Are we going to stick a needle into someone's brain and draw out some blood or fluid? I don't think so. Are we going to draw blood from the arm, which is far removed from the synaptic gap? That would not be helpful. Only 5 percent of the body's serotonin is found in the brain. The abundance of serotonin is in the rest of the body, mostly the stomach. Serotonin helps process food through the stomach. It also helps to control blood flow and clotting.[1]

Pharmaceutical companies test drugs like Prozac, Zoloft, Paxil, and Luvox to see if they can raise serotonin levels in depressed people. They do this by putting the drugs into rats. They then put the rat brains into a blender and chop them up into smaller pieces so they can examine the effects of their medications. Then they make a hypothesis as to the effect the drug might have in humans.[2]

The American Medical Association makes the following comments about serotonin: "Researchers are uncertain exactly why changing levels of neurotransmitters can lead to depression." "Researchers are also uncertain whether depressive illness results from or causes changes in the level of certain neurotransmitters. Some researchers think it works both ways."[3]

Dr. Glenmullen gives a very interesting observation about serotonin:

> A serotonin deficiency for depression has not been found. A pioneer in the search for one is the Dutch psychiatrist Herman van Praag. In his 1993 book *"Make-Believes" in Psychiatry,* van Praag traces the history of the search for serotonin imbalance. Initially, in the mid-1960s, van Praag and other researchers found a deficiency of a close chemical cousin of serotonin, called 5-HIAA, in the cerebrospinal fluid of some depressed patients. The work was suggestive of a serotonin deficiency but far from conclusive. Later researchers found similar suggestive but inconclusive deficiencies in patients with a wide range of diagnoses, including anxiety, personality disorders, and schizophrenia. For a time, researchers thought the deficiency might be indicative of suicidality rather than any specific psychiatric diagnosis. Eventually, however, this too proved not to be the case, as it was found in patients who were not suicidal but simply irritable, hostile, and aggressive. In the end, the deficiency proved neither diagnostic nor specific for any psychiatric condition. Still, patients are often given the impression that a definitive serotonin deficiency in depression is firmly established.[4]

Dr. Glenmullen also says,

> In recent decades, we have had no shortage of alleged biochemical imbalances for psychiatric conditions. Diligent though these attempts have been, not one has been proven. Quite the contrary. In every instance where such an imbalance was thought to have been found, it was later proven false.[5]

But for the sake of the argument, let's pretend that some kind of change in serotonin does occur. Does that change cause the depression or does the depression cause the change in serotonin? The latter is much more likely to be true. If I took you to a bridge, tied a bungee cord onto you, and threw you over the edge, what do you think would happen? Besides fighting me, yelling, and getting mad, you would experience extreme fear as you began to fall. Your breathing would change, and your entire body would be charged with adrenaline. (Adrenaline is released when we perceive any kind of fight or flight type of danger.) As you finally stopped bouncing up and down and we lowered you to the ground, you would notice something else. You would be shaking all over. That's the aftereffect of the adrenaline. After a while, your body system would be back to normal.

Now, let's ask the question: Did the adrenaline cause the experience of falling or did the experience of falling cause the surge of adrenaline? Of course, the answer is that the experience (the thought of danger or death) caused the adrenaline to flow. A change in the chemical balance in an individual is the result of the person's thinking and emotions, not the cause of them. This is a very strategic point. It will determine how you view depression and attempt to overcome it. If you truly believe that the lowering of serotonin causes depression, you will use drugs to try to chemically balance the body. If, however, you believe that the change in serotonin is caused by your perception of thoughts, events, and circumstances, you will not go for the drugs. You will attempt to deal with anxiety and depression by examining your thoughts and perceptions of what is happening in your life.

The Dark Side of Drugs

The next time you turn on the television, listen carefully to commercials advertising various drugs. Pay special note to the drugs' side effects. You may hear something like this: "Certain individuals may experience nausea, vomiting, and diarrhea. There may be a lessening of sexual desire…" The one that floors me says that in rare cases, individuals may experience lymphoma. Hello! You mean to tell me that you want to sell me a drug that could cause tumors in my body? I'm certainly going to rush out and buy that one. I can't wait for a tumor!

If you are going to consider taking any medications for your anxiety and depression, you need to know what you are getting into. Some medications can trigger depression or make it worse:

- illegal drugs
- alcohol
- antianxiety drugs like Valium and Zanax
- anticonvulsants like Dilantin and Tegretol

- antihistamines like Benadryl and Hismanal
- Parkinson's disease drugs like Dopar and Sinemet
- heart drugs like Cardizem and Inderal
- chemotherapy drugs like Velban and Oncovin
- corticosteroids like Cortone and Deltasone
- hormones like estrogen and progesterone

If you're dealing with anxiety or depression, it is very important that you explore the possibility that your emotions or mood changes are not tied to a physical ailment in your body. Listed below are some of the medical conditions that *could* be associated with the experience of anxiety and depression. You may wish to check these out with your medical doctor.

ANXIETY-RELATED MEDICAL CONDITIONS

Cardiovascular

acute myocardial infarction	angina pectoris
arrhythmias	congestive heart failure
hypertension	hypotension
ischemic heart disease	mitral valve prolapse
pericarditis	

Endocrinologic & Metabolic

carcinoid syndrome	Cushing's disease
diabetes	electrolyte imbalance
hypercalcemia	hypercalemia
hyperthyroidism	hypoglycemia
hyponatremia	parathyroid disease
pheochromocytoma	porphyria

Gastrointestinal

irritable bowel syndrome

Gynecologic

menopause	premenstrual dysphoric disorder

Hematologic

anaphylactic shock   anemia

chronic immune diseases

Neurologic

brain tumor   delirium

encephalopathy   epilepsy

essential tremor   familiar tremor

Parkinson's disease   seizure disorders

transient ischemic attack   vertigo

Respiratory

asthma   chronic obstructive pulmonary disease

emphysema   dyspnea (difficulty in breathing)

pulmonary edema   pulmonary embolus

SOURCE: *Patient Care* MAGAZINE, AUGUST 15, 1999, P. 82

DEPRESSION-RELATED MEDICAL CONDITIONS

Neurologic

Parkinson's disease   Huntington's disease

traumatic brain injury   stroke

dementias   multiple sclerosis

Metabolic

electrolyte disturbances   renal failure

vitamin deficiencies or excess   acute intermittent porphyria

Wilson's disease   environmental toxins

heavy metals

Gastrointestinal

irritable bowel syndrome   chronic pancreatitis

Crohn's disease   cirrhosis

hepatic encephalopathy

Endocrine

hypothyroidism	hyperthyroidism
Cushing's disease	Addison's disease
diabetes mellitus	parathyroid dysfunction

Cardiovascular

myocardial infarction angina　coronary artery bypass surgery

cardiomyopathies

Pulmonary

sleep apnea　chronic obstructive pulmonary disease

reactive airway disease

Malignancies and Hemotologic

pancreatic carcinoma	brain tumors
anemias	paraneoplastic syndromes

Autoimmune

fibromyalgia　systemic lupus erythematosus

rheumatoid arthritis

SOURCE: S.L. DUBOVSKY AND R. BUZAN, "MOOD DISORDERS," IN: R.E. HALES, S.C. YUDOFSKY, AND J.A. TALBOTT, EDS. *The American Psychiatric Press Textook of Psychiatry,* 3ʀᴅ ED. (WASHINGTON, DC: AMERICAN PSYCHIATRIC PRESS; 1999): 479-565.

Many side effects are associated with taking the major antianxiety and antidepression drugs. Strange outcomes can include muscle spasms and facial tics. The muscle spasms can be in the neck, shoulders, jaw, arms, and legs. Patients cannot stop or control these neurological side effects, such as...

- mild leg tapping
- Parkinson's-like symptoms
- acute spasms in the legs
- foot dragging
- involuntary wiggling of the toes
- irregular jerking moments in both arms and legs

A person on medication can also have strange and freakish facial tics.

- "Fly catching"—the tongue involuntarily thrusting in and out of the mouth
- "Bon-bon"—candy-sucking-like movements of the lips and tongue
- "Teeth darting"—involuntary tongue movements across the teeth
- Rapid eye blinking
- Severe clenching of the teeth
- Tremors in the lips
- Eyelid spasms[6]

A study being conducted at the Yale University School of Medicine has estimated that 32% of patients develop persistent tics after 5 years on major tranquilizers, 57% by 15 years, and 68% by 25 years.[7]

Additional research findings on drug side effects include things like excessive weight gain and sexual dysfunction.

Dr. Norman Sussman, Director of Psychopharmacology Research at Bellevue Hospital in New York, was quoted as saying that paradoxical weight gain was one of the most common, long-term side effects of the Prozac group now prompting patients to insist on going off the drugs.[8]

The *Southern Medical Journal to the American Journal of Psychiatry* suggests, "Studies revealed rates as high as 75% of patients on these drugs reporting sexual dysfunction."[9]

When comparing the use of psychotherapy to the use of drugs for treating and controlling depression, some interesting results surfaced.

At the end of two years, only 23% of the patients who had been treated with psychotherapy had relapsed. By contrast, 78% of those treated with only medication had had a return of depression. Similar studies of the treatment of anxiety disorders have shown psychological intervention more effective in the long run than medications.[10]

You may ask, "Are you saying that I should not take any medications for anxiety or depression?" That's a fair response. To answer that question, let me ask a few questions.

Do you think your anxiety or depression is tied to some circumstance in your life?

- Have you lost your job?
- Have you recently retired?
- Have you experienced financial losses?
- Have you been involved in an accident?
- Have you committed some criminal act?
- Have you been having marital problems?
- Are you facing an important decision?
- Have you been having troubles with in-laws?
- Have you been violated by some criminal act?
- Has a natural disaster destroyed your home or possessions?
- Do you have a conflict you need to deal with but are afraid to face?
- Have you lost a loved one through a broken relationship or a death?

Do you think that your anxiety or depression is tied to some medical or health related issues in your life?

- Have you had trouble sleeping?
- Have you had difficulty breathing?
- Have you been struggling with stomach disorders?
- Have you had a problem with diarrhea or constipation?
- Have you been experiencing a great deal of headaches?
- Have you noticed a lot of twitching and shaking in your body?

By all means, you should check out any problems that may be related to some health issue in your life. If you discover your anxiety or depression is not tied to a medical problem, what are you going to do? Are you

POSSIBLE SIDE EFFECTS
from the most popular mood-altering drugs on the market

Choose the side effects you would like to experience!

Abdominal pain
Abnormal dreams
Abnormal ejaculation
Abnormal eye movements
Abnormal thinking
Aching
Acne
Acute anxiety reaction
Acute dystonia (sudden muscle stiffness)
Addiction
Agitation
Anger
Anorexia
Arrhythmias
Back pain
Bloating
Blurred vision
Bone marrow depressions
Breast enlargement
Cardiac arrest
Catatonia
Central nervous system depression
Chest congestion
Chills
Clumsiness

Coma
Concentration difficulties
Confusion
Constipation
Coughing
Cramps
Decreased appetite
Decreased movement
Decreased sex drive
Decreased thyroid gland functioning
Dehydration
Delusions
Depression
Diarrhea
Difficulty urinating
Disorientation
Dizziness
Drowsiness
Dry mouth
Eczema
Ejaculatory failure
Excessive appetite
Excitement
Faintness
Fatigue
Fear
Fever
Flu syndrome
Gastrointestinal complaints
Hair loss
Hallucinations
Hand tremors

Headaches
High abuse potential
High sedative effects
Hypertension
Hypomania
Hypotension
Hypoventilation
Impotence
Increased appetite
Increased duration of sleep
Increased salivation and drooling
Increased sensitivity to the sun
Increased sweating
Infection
Insomnia
Involuntary movements of the tongue, jaw, trunk, or extremities
Irregular pulse
Irritability
Jumpiness
Lethargy
Lightheadedness
Loss of motivation
Loss of sex drive
Mania
Menstrual irregularities
Mental confusion
Metallic taste in mouth
Migraines
Muscle weakness
Myocardial infarction
Nausea
Nervousness

Neurological impairments
Neuromuscular reactions
Nightmares
Numbness of limbs
Palpitations
Panic
Paranoia
Parkinson's syndrome (tremors and muscle stiffness)
Poor concentration
Postural hypotension
Psychosis
Rapid pulse rate
Sedation
Seizures
Shortness of breath
Skin rash
Slurred speech
Somnolence
Sores in mouth
Staggering
Stroke
Testicular swelling
Tingling
Tremors
Unsteadiness
Urinary frequency
Vivid dreams
Vomiting
Weakness
Weight gain
Weight loss
Worry

going to convince yourself that you have some type of chemical imbalance? Keep in mind that about only 5 percent of anxiety and depression cases are influenced by medical issues. The talk of chemical imbalance *causing* anxiety and depression is just that—it's talk. It is an unproven theory. The vast majority of anxiety and depression is influenced by our perceptions of the circumstances and events in our lives.

Medications do not change any circumstances or events. If you have lost your job or you are going through a divorce, drugs may dull your senses or give you a little euphoria for a little while. They will not, however, get you your job back or restore your marriage. The question then arises, why are you taking the medications? Is it to hide from the reality of what is happening in your life? Are you seeking some kind of escape from the emotional pain you are feeling? Granted, you might get a temporary relief, but are you then trading momentary relief for long-term dependency on drugs? Is that what you really want to accomplish?

Throughout human history, men and women have encountered trials and difficulties in their lives. Trouble and misery are common to all people. Most fiction books and biographies recount the difficulties and obstacles people overcame. We read their stories or see their lives depicted in movies or on television. We identify with their hurt and pain. We are encouraged by their courage and tenacity. We are inspired and challenged to follow their model of overcoming adversity. Why then do we want to rely on drugs or alcohol in the face of a crisis in our lives? Why can't we too rise to the occasion as they did? Why can't we agree not to throw in the towel and give up?

Someone may respond, "But you don't realize all the hurt and pain I have experienced. You don't know all the issues I'm facing. I don't think I can continue any longer. My energy is gone, and I'm at the end of my string."

I suggest that you can do more than you think you can. The human spirit is stronger than most people know. I'm reminded of the story told by Dr. Jay Adams.

> I once drove through the Garden of the Gods outside Colorado Springs. In this beautiful natural wonder you can see rocks balanced on a pinpoint and vividly colored scenery on all sides. As you drive along slowly, viewing the marvels about you, suddenly you are confronted with a problem: directly ahead of

you looms a wall of sheer rock, and the road on which you are traveling disappears into what seems to be a crack so narrow that it looks as though you'd have a hard time driving a VW through it. Looking around for a place in which to turn and go back, you eye falls on a small white sign. It reads,

—Narrows—
Yes you can.
A Million Others Have

and what do you know—a minute and a half later, a million and one have done it.[11]

I want to encourage you. You are not alone. Millions of other people are going through similar difficulties. The way has been narrow for them too. They have learned how to overcome their anxiety and depression, and so can you. I think you can do it without medication or at least with very little medication. What do you think? Do you want to give it a try?

8

The DISRUPTED MIND
Your Choices and Your Mental Health

❖ ❖ ❖

The beauty of the soul shines out when a man bears with
composure one heavy mischance after another,
not because he does not feel them but because
he is a man of high and heroic temper.

ARISTOTLE

SOME INTERESTING INSIGHTS ABOUT human nature can be gained from an ancient Middle Eastern book—the Bible. Although it is not a psychological textbook or a manual on mental health, it does touch on these subjects. It suggests the source of personal conflicts, negative interpersonal relationships, and inappropriate thoughts and behavior.

For example, James, the brother of Jesus, talks about dealing with negative thoughts and behaviors. He refers to them as temptations. Have you ever been tempted to lie, steal, or get revenge? Have you been tempted to explode with anger, develop bitterness, or wallow in your misery and feel sorry for yourself? Have you been tempted to tell someone off, think that life is unfair, or harbor unforgiveness? Have you been tempted to commit suicide, get upset with God, or just give up?

> Blessed is the man who endures temptation; for when he has been approved, he will receive the crown of life which the Lord has promised to those who love Him. Let no one say when he is tempted, "I am tempted by God"; for God cannot be tempted by evil, nor does He Himself tempt anyone. But each one is tempted when he is drawn away by his own desires

and enticed. Then, when desire has conceived, it gives birth to sin; and sin, when it is full-grown, brings forth death (James 1:12-15 NKJV).

The truth of the matter is that everyone is born with natural impulses and desires. We don't have to teach children how to lie, steal, cheat, or get into fights. We don't have to teach them the phrase "That's mine!" Expressing hostility and selfishness and throwing temper tantrums are inborn and effortless for them. Developing character and learning principles for healthy living, on the other hand, have to be modeled and taught. They come through repetition, struggle, and hard work.

In recent years, our society has changed dramatically. We no longer talk about character, conviction, and moral obligation. We instead discuss the emerging self and our need for coping mechanisms. Living by principles has given way to living within the boundaries of my mental health diagnosis. The goal for life seems to be the satisfaction of the needs of the individual.

What will happen to the individual, and to society in general, if people think only about their own needs rather than the needs of others? Where does accountability and responsibility for our actions come into play? Living by principles adds stability and continuity. Principles give purpose and direction and provide the impetus for enduring the hard times of life. Without principles, individuals become totally selfish, and society disintegrates.

If people attend counseling or check into rehab believing that their problem is a disease or an illness, they are absolved of personal responsibility. The illness has caused their difficulties. They are just victims.

Most medical doctors have been highly trained to discover, diagnose, and treat medical illness. They do this by recommending a change in diet, exercise, rest, medications, and/or surgery. But what about mental disorders?

> Everyone must overcome problems, difficulties, and trials. When they do, they experience peace and happiness. So where do emotional temptations and thoughts come from? They come from negative and unproductive thinking patterns. When we entertain these thoughts long enough, they give birth to actions. Thoughts and actions give rise to a lifestyle and eventually to our destiny.

We previously alluded to a book called the *Diagnostic and Statistical Manual of Mental Disorders* (DSM-IV). It is designed to help doctors and mental health practitioners identify and classify various forms and degrees of mental illness or mental disease. Listed below are a number of these disorders mentioned in the DSM-IV. You may be amazed to discover that no medical cure exists for the following dysfunctions.

- alcohol addiction
- anorexia nervosa
- anxiety
- bereavement
- bipolar disorder
- bulimia nervosa
- caffeine addiction
- dependent personality disorder
- depression
- exhibitionism
- explosive disorder
- fetishism
- gambling addiction
- gender identity disorder
- impulse control disorder
- kleptomania
- malingering
- masochism
- most sleep disorders
- narcissistic personality disorder
- negativistic personality disorder
- obsessive compulsive disorder
- panic disorders
- phobias
- post-traumatic stress disorder
- pyromania
- sadism

- sexual addictions
- trichotillomania
- voyeurism

Regardless of what the media suggest, regardless of what the psychological community has accepted, and regardless of what we want to believe, the illnesses and diseases listed above cannot be cured by the medical profession. The reason is that they are not illnesses and diseases in the first place. They are dysfunctions caused by thinking processes and by behavior choices.

Jesus alluded to this concept. His disciples had been inundated by crowds of people who made demands on them. Jesus led the group into a house to escape and get some peace and quiet. Outside of the home they had been discussing the concept of Jewish customs regarding washing before meals, what you eat, and following Jewish laws.

> Then Jesus called to the crowd to come and hear. "All of you listen," he said, "and try to understand. You are not defiled by what you eat; you are defiled by what you say and do!"
>
> Then Jesus went into a house to get away from the crowds, and his disciples asked him what he meant by the statement he had made. "Don't you understand either?" he asked. "Can't you see that what you eat won't defile you? Food doesn't come in contact with your heart, but only passes through the stomach and then comes out again." (By saying this, he showed that every kind of food is acceptable.)
>
> And then he added, "It is the thought-life that defiles you. For from within, out of a person's heart, come evil thoughts, sexual immorality, theft, murder, adultery, greed, wickedness, deceit, eagerness for lustful pleasure, envy, slander, pride, and foolishness. All these vile things come from within; they are what defile you and make you unacceptable to God" (Mark 7:14-23 NLT).

We have all been given the power to choose, and we make numerous choices every day. We decide what time to get up in the morning, what we'll eat for breakfast, what to wear to work or school, whether or not to take our cell phone with us, which freeway to drive…and a host of other decisions. Finally, we decide what time to go to bed and if we'll read or watch television till we fall asleep.

When we go to a restaurant we choose to eat steak rather than spaghetti. When we buy a car we choose to drive a Toyota pickup or a Mustang. Or a Hummer might be nice. When we turn on our computers we decide which Internet sites we'll enter.

Of course, those are only mundane, everyday choices. However, you also have the power to make more important and morally profound choices. You can choose not to steal oranges from the tree in your neighbor's yard. You can choose to obey the speed limit. You can choose not to steal time or take materials from your employer. You can choose not to lie to your children or your spouse.

> Regardless of circumstances, each man lives in a world of his own making.
>
> JOSEPHA MURRAY EMMS

You can choose not to abuse your family. You can choose not to commit adultery with your neighbor's spouse. You can choose not to embezzle money from a fund-raising project you're involved with.

You also have a choice to get mad at someone or let the matter roll off your back. You have the choice to forgive people or hold bitterness and resentment against them. You have the choice to yell and throw a temper tantrum or be calm and gentle. Heavy-duty choices like these have a profound effect in your life.

By way of personal example, let me share a story. A number of years ago my wife and I were approached by a Christian businessman to invest in a real estate subdivision. We were told that our investment would be secured by the land and that we could not lose any money because the land could always be sold and the investment regained. We personally knew the businessman and trusted him. The project sounded very stable, and the clincher was that we were buying the land and our names would be on the property. You can sense what is coming.

Some time passed, and the housing market began to drop. We were not uncomfortable because we had our names on the land and not in buildings. Little did we know that this individual did not put our names on the land, nor did he use our funds to purchase the land. He had leveraged our monies, along with money from other people, to fund a separate subdivision he was building.

Our investment was part of $4 million that was lost in this venture. Our contribution was $70,000 that we borrowed on our home. I now respond to people who want to encourage me to invest in this or that project, "All I need now is one more good deal, and I'll be bankrupt."

Speaking of bankruptcy, I don't believe in it. Because of that conviction, I began to pay back the borrowed money on a monthly basis. It took 17 long years to pay off that decision.

Now, let me ask the question. Do you think I encountered any anxious moments during those 17 years? Do you think I was depressed because of what had occurred? You know the answer. Along with the anxiety and depression came anger. I was angry with the man who was dishonest with our money and others'. I was angry with how stupid I had been to put my family in financial jeopardy.

I had a 17-year monthly reminder of the pain of this decision. I eventually realized that I had to let go of the anger I was feeling and the depression I was experiencing. I did that. I chose to forgive the individual. However, even though I forgave him, I was continually bombarded by the monthly reminder from the bank. I still had to pay the money back. What changed? Only my attitude about what had happened. I had learned a great lesson. An expensive one to say the least, but still a lesson in wisdom, emotional health, and the freedom that comes with forgiving those who harm us. The memory of that loss is still with me, but the pain of the loss has been removed. And that's a good thing. I can live with that.

On the other hand, I could have chosen not to forgive him. I could have burned with anger and resentment. I could have attempted to seek some form of revenge and get even with him. I could have become a bitter person.

Why then do we believe that we are victims and have no power of choice over anxiety and depression? Do we not choose to dwell on upsetting thoughts and play them over and over in our minds until concern turns to worry, and worry grows into anxiety? Do we not choose to ruminate over past hurts and events like a cow vomiting up its cud and chewing it over and over again? To overcome anxiety and depression we must reject thoughts that destroy our joy and make us emotionally unhealthy.

Overcoming negative and unhealthy thinking is not an easy task. Somehow our discouraged feelings do not want to give up their influence and control over us. We struggle to work our way back from the valley of despair to the path that leads up the mountain of happiness.

Making a decision to change our thinking requires much effort. This is especially true when we are facing some sort of crisis in our life. The fear of making the wrong decision causes procrastination and laziness. At this point we need courage.

Courage takes many forms. There is physical courage, there is moral courage. Then there is a still higher type of courage—the courage to brave pain, to live with it, to never let others know of it, and to still find joy in life; to wake up in the morning with enthusiasm for the day ahead.

HOWARD COSELL

In tough times we must simply bite the bullet. I'm sure you have heard this phrase before, but do you know where it came from? When wounded American Civil War soldiers were brought to the doctors, some of them had to have arms or legs amputated. When the doctors ran out of anesthetics to deaden pain, they put the soft lead of a bullet between the teeth of the patient. The doctor then said, "Grit your teeth and bite the bullet." The soldier would bite down and scream as the doctor cut off his arm or leg. It was not a pleasant experience.

The same is true in our lives. Sometimes we have to bite the bullet when our emotions scream with pain. No one enjoys facing difficult issues, but sometimes an amputation has to take place. Often we have to face our fears and angers before healing can occur.

Are you worried about money and paying your bills? How about biting the bullet and cutting back on unnecessary purchases? How about taking a second part-time job? How about working harder? No pill will bring about financial success.

Are you anxious about relationships and being loved? How about biting the bullet and smiling for a change? How about being kind? How about making yourself more giving and lovable? No drug can heal a broken heart.

Are you afraid of losing your job? How about biting the bullet and being to work on time and not taking long breaks? How about seeking to make your boss' job easier? How about coming up with creative suggestions rather than constant complaints? How about striving to make yourself indispensable? No medicine will give you a new career.

What would happen if we redirected our energy away from worry, anxiety, and depression and toward a solution? How about biting the bullet and spending time planning a positive course for change? How about looking at your problems with a new set of eyes? How about changing your outlook from despair to hopefulness and positiveness?

Is brooding about problems and difficulties the way to solve them? Will inactivity make your difficulties go away? Will taking pills solve the turmoil in your life? Do you really need to depend on doctors and psychologists for your happiness?

> "Neurotic" means he is not as sensible as I am, and "psychotic" means he's worse than my brother-in-law.
>
> KARL MENNINGER

Before doctors and psychologists created a host of psychological terms like "neurosis" and "psychosis," how did people deal with difficulty and tragedy? How did they cope with disappointment and discouragement?

They listened to the time-tested advice of their family and friends. They took various "emotional pills," like these:

- Keep busy.
- Get on with life.
- Don't dwell on it.
- Start exercising.
- Get out of the house.
- Go sit in the sunshine.
- Throw yourself into your work.
- Accept what you cannot change.
- Start helping others who are worse off.
- Read the book of Psalms.

In earlier times, adversity and difficulty helped men and women develop and improve their character. Suffering was a real and valid part of the human experience. People understood that to deny or run from that fact would be detrimental to developing mature mental health.

Pain has a message attached to it that we should embrace rather than reject. We can learn lessons from our trials and hard times. We will never be able to eliminate them from our lives, so we do well to draw out experience and wisdom from these pressures.

You can choose to view suffering as something that destroys you or something that makes you stronger. Your struggles can make you sensitive to the needs and feelings of others who are encountering similar experiences.

Rather than looking for the causes of anxiety and depression, we might be wiser to look for the meaning in them.

Focusing on the *why* of life requires very little effort and action. Why am I feeling this way? Why is this happening to me? Why can't life be different? Many of the why questions can never be answered to our satisfaction.

On the other hand, if I turn my focus on the *how* of life, change can begin. How do I feel about what is happening to me? How can I get some help? How can I learn from this? How can I make positive changes in my situation? How can I change my attitude? As I examine the how of life, I take on responsibility for making change.

The Old Testament character Job experienced far more adversity than most people will ever experience. If anyone had a right to be anxious or depressed, he certainly did. After he lost most of his financial wealth, his children were killed, and he encountered massive illness, his loving wife suggested that he should curse God and commit suicide. His attitude and response is most instructive.

> Then his wife said to him, "Do you still hold fast your integrity? Curse God and die!" But he said to her, "You speak as one of the foolish women speaks. Shall we indeed accept good from God and not accept adversity?" In all this Job did not sin with his lips (Job 2:9-10 NASB).

How are you doing with accepting the adversity in your life? Are you trusting God in your situation? Or, are you considering the advice of Job's wife—to curse God and die?

9

The RECEPTIVE MIND
Taking Control of Your Fears

❖ ❖ ❖

*Words can never adequately convey the incredible impact
of our attitude toward life. The longer I live the more
convinced I become that life is 10 percent what happens to
us and 90 percent how we respond to it.*

CHARLES SWINDOLL

"I NEED YOUR HELP," SAID TRINA. I could see her lips slightly tremble as she fiddled with a Kleenex in her hands. Her brown eyes were watery and her tears were about to spill over her eyelids. "I think I'm going crazy. I'm so worried about my job and my future that I can't think straight. I have a hard time getting to sleep. I keep waking up around three each morning. I have so much turmoil, I can't go back to sleep. I'm so tired and out of energy. I just want to escape. My depression is growing daily, and I can't see any way out. Can you give me a pill or do something quick to help me?"

Wouldn't it be nice if it were that easy? But the truth is that most problems in life do not come overnight, and they probably won't leave overnight. Wishful thinking and instant easy answers are not quite that simple.

Our society is filled with microwave thinking. Everything must happen instantly. We have instant breakfast meals, fast-food restaurants, and television news interviews that are less than a minute long. Political speeches are quoted in 15-second sound bites. We even have counseling television programs where problems seem to be resolved between commercials.

To be sure, some issues in life are common to all men and women. They involve things like health, finances, career, family, sexuality, religion, relationships, and relatives. But even though similar threads run through many problems, each individual case is unique, and particular circumstances vary like fingerprints.

Everybody experiences the feelings of anxiety and depression at some time or other. The degree and depth of the anxiety and depression vary according to the individual and his or her particular situation.

Many books have been written about anxiety and depression. Some people have asked me, "Can you have anxiety without depression?" The answer is yes. Others have asked, "Can you have depression without anxiety?" The answer is yes. I have chosen to put them together because they are often two sides to the same coin. Many people experience both of them.

In fact, when anxiety is added to depression, depression grows deeper and more substantial. The anxiety acts like fertilizer and enhances the growth of detrimental thinking. It also promotes the spread of the weeds of worry.

When we talk about how to identify, cope with, and overcome anxiety and depression, I will not generally separate the two issues. The reason for this is that most of the suggestions will help with both. For example, thinking positive thoughts will help control both anxiety and depression.

You may recall in the beginning of the book that I suggested that anxiety usually comes from fear of the unknown and fear of the future. Conversely, depression usually arises out of past hurts and losses. Often anger is the baby that is born from the painful circumstances. Our inability to change the past or determine the future causes a great deal

Major Fears

Fear of the unknown
   We want guarantees.

Fear of failure
   We don't want to be wrong.

Fear of rejection
   We want to be liked by everyone.

Fear of commitment
   We resist responsibility.

Fear of success
   We don't want to set too high a standard that we must continually exceed.

of mental turmoil in our thinking. We then have a tendency to lose perspective on life.

I also mentioned that a common thread runs through anxiety and depression. These emotions seem to be attempts for us to gain control of what we cannot always control—the past or the future. Our inability to control the events in our lives creates fears and gives rise to anger. Whether we like it or not, the desire to control is woven into the fabric of our personalities. We all want things done the way we would like and in the time we like. When we perceive that things are not going our way, we become fearful, anxious, angry, and depressed. We may even sulk, whine, or throw a temper tantrum in our attempt to exert control over the circumstance.

Indeed, we *should* be concerned about certain issues in life. We want to protect our children from harm and danger. We instruct them not to run into the street because a car could hit them. This is good, right, and proper parenting. However, legitimate concern for their welfare can turn into worry. If our children go over to a friend's house to play, they're no longer under our supervision and control. They might run out into the street at the friend's house. If we sit at home and think about this possible danger to our children long enough, our concern can distort into worry. Conscious worry can be twisted and warped into a free-floating anxiety that overwhelms us. The anxiety is hard for us to cope with and understand because it contains multiple worries.

Why do these fears and worries overwhelm us? Because the things we are worrying about are out of our control. We act as if we want to be God and make all the proper decisions for our lives. We make an important step when we realize that we are not God and that we must accept certain events in our lives regardless of whether we want them or like them. We need to acknowledge that all of our fears, worries, anxieties, angers, and depression will not solve or accomplish anything. That is a step toward maturity and growth.

May I emphasize that point by asking you some personal questions? Has your worry helped you? Does your anxiety keep problems away? Has the depression you've been feeling changed your circumstances? If what you've been doing is not working, why continue it? The comic strip character Charlie Brown mentioned that he had developed a new philosophy; "I only dread one day at a time."

God has given us the emotions of fear and anger. Fear helps us to flee from situations that would be unsafe or unhealthy for us. Anger gives us the ability to fight and protect ourselves from harmful people or circumstances. Fear is not a disease, it's simply fear. Anger is not an illness, it's merely anger. The same can be said for anxiety—it is not an illness. It's only confused and unfocused thinking. And depression is not a sickness. It's usually a collection of memories and feelings centering on hurts and losses. Many people say, "I'm depressed." A more responsible approach would be to say, "I'm in the process of depressing," or "I'm in the process of being anxious." This approach takes ownership for our thought life.

In this book I have chosen not to focus on medication as the major method of dealing with anxiety and depression. This is not because medication could not possibly be beneficial in some cases. It's because tons of books have been written on the use of medication for anxiety and depression. I strongly disagree with their emphasis because drugs only blur, mask, and ignore the real causes for most anxiety and depression.

Drug therapies do not improve your self-image, heal broken relationships, or teach you life-coping skills. They do not eliminate stress in your life, take hurt and loss from your life, or change your negative focus on yourself. They do not help you to take responsibility for your own mental health, and they can have detrimental side effects to your health and can make you drug dependent.

I have also chosen to place little emphasis on vitamins, diet, and preparation of foods. This is not because I don't think that what you eat helps to determine your general fitness. Diet is extremely important, not only for mental well-being but also for all-around physical health. The B-complex vitamins are essential for helping us to deal with stress. However, you can easily find a plethora of books about the proper foods to eat and how they affect your thinking and emotions. I would encourage you to purchase books that will help you choose the proper foods for healthy living.

My personal belief is that we have access to an overabundant amount of writing about drugs and diet for the treatment of anxiety and depression. The glut of drug-related literature hasn't seemed to slow the amount of anxiety and depression people are experiencing. It also hasn't slowed the increase of the profits drug companies are making off of hurting people.

I am fully aware that you may be on some form of medication for your anxiety or depression. You may have found some relief from how you were feeling. But is your use of drugs for the short term or for the long haul?

Are you dependent on them? Can you not function without them? Are you happy about the side effects, especially the sexual side effects a great majority of people experience to some degree? I am not suggesting you should stop your medication "cold turkey." That could prove to be very detrimental for you.

My concern is this: How is the rest of your life doing? Are you happy? Are your interpersonal relationships clear and healthy? Are you facing the future with hope and excitement? Is your financial house in order? Is your family functioning well? Are you exercising and sleeping as much as you know you need to and would like to do? Is your conscience clear, and do you feel guilt free? Do you have clear goals for the future, or are you lonely and bored? How are you doing spiritually? Do you feel empty, as if something is missing?

A number of years ago, the actress Patty Duke wrote a book entitled *A Brilliant Madness* describing her battle with depression. She began the book by saying, "A disease, thank God!" In essence, she was grateful she finally discovered the source of all of her sadness—she had an illness or disease. I would like to turn her phrase around. "Thank God, it's not a disease!"

The DSM-IV mentions many different phobias under the heading of Anxiety Disorders. The implication is that they are some form of mental illness. One of the phobias is entomophobia—the fear of bugs and insects. How do you do with insects? Do they get to you? Or can you take them or leave them?

When I was a young boy, our home was in Denver, Colorado. I didn't realize at the time that my parents were moderately poor. We lived in the basement of my mother's parents' home. We lived with my grandparents for about ten years before my parents could afford to buy their own home.

The basement included the heater room. The heater burned coal that was stored in a large cement bin outside the house. A metal chute allowed the coal to drop into the heater room. Along with the coal came insects known as centipedes. Centipedes have a pair of long antennae on their heads that wiggle back and forth as they feel their way around. They also have two sets of jaws. A full-grown centipede has up to 170 pairs of legs and can be two to three inches long. The first pair of legs, behind the head, has claws for fighting rather than walking. These claws are called "poison claws." They are filled with poison from a gland in the centipede's head.

Centipedes scurry very rapidly across the floor and up the walls and on the ceiling. They are not the most attractive creature in God's creation. They give me the willies.

The bedroom my brother and I slept in was next to the heater room. In fact, we had to pass through the heater room to get to our bedroom. As I passed through the heater room, I began to develop a fear of centipedes. They were all over the room. I don't think I was afraid of them at first. I think the fear emerged when my older brother informed me that centipedes love to run up your body and go for your ears. He told me they eat the wax out of your ears.

That did it for me. I always ran through the heater room into our bedroom. I certainly didn't want those creatures eating out of my head. According to the books, I guess I had a mental illness. I had a phobia of centipedes. It didn't come from a virus, bacteria, or protozoa. It came from my response to my brother's word picture.

As I grew older I realized that I had nothing to fear from centipedes. They really don't have a thing for earwax. As I corrected the information in my head and began to think proper thoughts about centipedes, the fear of those insects disappeared. And with the fear, the so-called mental illness disappeared also.

As you read this, I'm sure that it sounds rather foolish. But I can assure you that from the time I was four until I was twelve, it wasn't foolish to me. Thoughts and perceptions are amazingly powerful even when they have no basis in fact. Our perceptions regulate our feelings and behaviors. False perceptions, misunderstandings, and a lack of information are not illnesses. Isn't that good news? Thank God, it's not a disease.

The Crooked Man

There was a crooked man,
And he walked a crooked mile,
He found a crooked sixpence
Upon a crooked stile;
He bought a crooked cat,
Which caught a crooked mouse,
And they all lived together
In a crooked little house.

My guess is that the crooked man also had crooked thoughts. His crooked thinking led him to live in the crooked house. It follows that crooked thinking leads to crooked living. Crooked living leads to a crooked lifestyle. He was probably even buried in a crooked little grave.

My desire is that we will change our crooked thinking about anxiety and depression to straight thinking, and that our straight thinking will lead to a straight lifestyle. Maybe we won't have to be bent over anymore by fears, worries, guilt, bitterness, or unforgiveness. I think standing straight and tall might feel good.

People travel to wonder at the height of mountains, at the huge waves of the sea, at the long courses of rivers, at the vast compass of the ocean, at the circular motion of the stars, and they pass by themselves without wondering.

AUGUSTINE

10

The REFLECTIVE MIND

Actions That Lead to Wholeness

❖ ❖ ❖

We are always in the forge or on the anvil;
by trials God is shaping us for higher things.

HENRY WARD BEECHER

TERRENCE HAD BEEN CRYING off and on for most of the week. Mornings were the worst time of the day for him. When he woke up, the reality of what happened overwhelmed him. Terrence had recently returned from the war. A rocket-propelled grenade had hit his armored vehicle, and two of his fellow soldiers were instantly blown apart. Terrence had lived through the event, but the doctors had to amputate both of his legs. He was suffering from what is called endogenous depression.

Endogenous depression can be caused by brain disorders, nervous system malfunction, infection, illness, chemical disturbance, accident, and injury. The shock of becoming a disabled person was very difficult for Terrence to adjust to. He had hopes and dreams that did not include this terrible set of circumstances. He went into a deep depression for several months.

Endogenous depression can be connected to an accident or injury, but more often it is caused by other changes in the body. These may include...

- *Menopause.* Women can feel distraught, irritable, impatient, and angry.

- *Giving birth.* Depression sometimes occurs after the birth of a child. Women with this depression may weep a lot, feel tense, and refuse food. They can feel anxious and fearful that something will happen to their newborn baby. Some are fearful that they might harm their own child.

- *Senility.* Older men and women may exhibit various behaviors, from whimpering to abusive outbursts of anger. Often their appetite will decrease. This can occur in some stages of Alzheimer's.

- *Infections.* Individuals with infections may be agitated and display weakness and mood disturbances. They may weep more frequently.

- *Drug use.* Certain medications can cause stupor, restlessness, extreme agitation, anger, and dysfunctional and irrational behaviors.

- *Brain injuries.* These can be caused by birth defects, accident, injury, or strokes. Thinking can become distorted, people may lose control of their emotions, and normal behaviors can become altered and strange.

- *Glandular disorders.* Emotional changes can be caused by dysfunctions of the thyroid gland, the pituitary gland, endocrine glands, the adrenal glands, diabetes, hypoglycemia, and other disturbances.

The family and friends of people with endogenous depression often understand why a person might be depressed if he or she was in an accident and lost a limb. They can put themselves in the person's place and imagine how they would think and feel. But what troubles many families is the depression that comes from within because of menopause, giving birth, senility, infections, toxic drugs, brain injuries, and glandular disorders. These are extremely difficult to understand and cope with. The depressed individual is chronically tired, shows almost no energy, and has almost no reserve strength. The depressed person often withdraws from family and friends. He has zero motivation and doesn't seem to care about anything. Because these disorders are beyond the comprehension of almost everyone, family and friends can become confused, impatient, and irritated. They can become upset with the depressed individual and with the doctors that have trouble helping the individual out of depression.

Some depression is created from the above causes. However, these are not where the majority of depression comes from. The overwhelming amount of depression arises from what we will call exogenous and erratic depression.

Exogenous depression comes from causes outside of the individual's body. This type of depression is also called reactive depression or grief depression. It may be the result of the loss of a loved one through death. Everyone at some time will experience grief at the loss of a friend or a family member. This is natural and normal. When the normal grieving depression turns into long-term bereavement, something else may be going on. It could indicate that the grieving person is an extremely dependent individual and has a difficult time functioning without the deceased. It could indicate extreme guilt for something that he or she should have said or done before the other person passed away. Or something may have been hidden from the individual who died, and the survivor has a guilty conscience. The depressed person may be angry at the individual that died. The deceased person may have left the survivor with a huge debt. The survivor may have to sell a home to repay creditors.

Exogenous depression can also come from other losses:

- the loss of a marriage through separation or divorce
- the loss of health due to an accident, injury, or illness like cancer or a heart attack
- the loss of a job
- the loss of finances and the mounting of bills
- the loss of material possessions due to some catastrophe like fire, flood, or hurricane
- the loss of face due to some embarrassing situation
- the loss of reputation
- the loss of recognition for a job well done when someone else gets the credit
- the loss of usefulness and the ability to make a contribution
- the loss of family and friends due to geographical uprooting and displacement
- the loss of belonging to some group

Exogenous depression is a little easier for family and friends to understand. This is because they too have experienced losses and stresses. They can empathize with the depressed person. Often the family and friends give support, comfort, and encouragement. People seem to be more warm and protective for people with this type of depression.

The third type of depression we are calling erratic depression. This is because it has a number of variables to it. It also ranges from mild to severe.

One of the major features of this type of depression is that the individual often feels like a victim. Another feature of erratic depression is the presence of damaged relationships. This comes from conflict and quarrels at home, at work, and with neighbors. The response from family and friends can vary from a mixture of pity and sympathy to extreme annoyance. Someone might tell the depressed person, "Oh, snap out of it!"

Erratic depression can arise from many sources.

- fears and anxieties
- panic thoughts and behaviors
- fear of social interaction with others
- low self-image and inferiority complex
- perfectionism
- obsessive-compulsive behaviors
- psychosomatic illnesses
- a hostile personality that has a difficult time getting along with others
- self-destructive behaviors like drug or alcohol abuse or criminal activity
- guilt for violations of a person's conscience
- back-and-forth mood swings brought about by what is commonly called bipolar disorder

Erratic depression is often the result of prolonged stress, loss of sleep, poor diet, lack of exercise, failure to achieve personal strivings, and anger over things not going your way. It can include anger over past wrongs and fear about future challenges. Unspoken and unfulfilled expectations, too much television, boredom, lack of purpose, not accepting responsibility, inability to adjust to hurtful experiences, and an unforgiving spirit can also be involved.

If we are honest with ourselves, we can easily see that most anxiety and depression are not based on a chemical imbalance that forces us to act and respond inappropriately. They usually come from mental battles within ourselves about what is good and bad, what is proper and improper, and what is responsible behavior and irresponsible behavior. This gives us hope because we can choose our responses to the difficulties of life.

In Romans 7:15-23, the apostle Paul addresses this battle between what we should be doing in life and what we actually end up doing:

> I don't understand myself at all, for I really want to do what is right, but I can't. I do what I don't want to—what I hate. I know perfectly well that what I am doing is wrong, and my bad conscience proves that I agree with these laws I am breaking. But I can't help myself because I'm no longer doing it. It is sin inside me that is stronger than I am that makes me do these evil things.
>
> I know I am rotten through and through so far as my old sinful nature is concerned. No matter which way I turn I can't make myself do right. I want to but I can't. When I want to do good, I don't; and when I try not to do wrong, I do it anyway. Now if I am doing what I don't want to, it is plain where the trouble is: sin still has me in its evil grasp.
>
> It seems to be a fact of life that when I want to do what is right, I inevitably do what is wrong. I love to do God's will so far as my new nature is concerned; but there is something else deep within me, in my lower nature, that is at war with my mind and wins the fight and makes me a slave to the sin that is still within me. In my mind I want to be God's willing servant, but instead I find myself still enslaved to sin.
>
> So you see how it is: my new life tells me to do right, but the old nature that is still inside me loves to sin. Oh, what a terrible predicament I'm in! Who will free me from my slavery to this deadly lower nature? Thank God! It has been done by Jesus Christ our Lord. He has set me free.

Life Rewards Action

Life does not compensate us for insight, understanding, wisdom, or intention. It only rewards action. I can tell the Internal Revenue Service that I intended to pay my taxes, but all they care about is the money. I can tell my wife that I understand how tired she is, but she would appreciate me more if I washed the dishes. I can tell my mechanic that I have gained much insight as to how an internal combustion engine runs, but all he will ask is "Did you put oil in it?" I can tell my children that I read a book and acquired much wisdom on being a father, but all they care about is whether I attended their soccer game. Henry Ford said, "You can't build a reputation on what you intend to do." It is so easy to get wrapped up in mind games and forget practical, daily living. We have to have the desire to change our thinking and behavior.

I am reminded of a story that James MacDonald shares in his book *I Really Want to Change…So, Help Me God*. It is the story of Raynald, who was a fourteenth-century duke in Belgium. Raynald eventually became the king of Belgium, but his brother Edward was very jealous. Edward convinced a group to follow him, and they overthrew Raynald's kingship. But Edward had compassion for Raynald and did not put him to death. Instead, he designed a special dungeon for him. It was a large circular room with one regular-sized doorway. It was outfitted with a bed, a table, and a chair. He included all the essentials that Raynald needed to be fairly comfortable.

When the dungeon was completely built *around* Raynald, Edward paid him a visit. Edward pointed to the regular-sized doorway and called Raynald's attention to the fact that there was no door in the opening. A door was not necessary to keep Raynald in the dungeon because he was grossly overweight and too fat to squeeze through the opening. Edward then said to Raynald, "When you can fit through the doorway, you can leave."

King Edward then instructed his servants to bring massive platters of meats and other delicacies and daily place them on the table in Raynald's round dungeon room. The servants also filled the table with various kinds of pies and pastries. Many people accused Edward of being cruel, but he responded, "My brother is not a prisoner. He can leave when he chooses to."

Now for the rest of the story:

> Raynald remained in that same room, a prisoner of his own appetite, for more than ten years. He wasn't released until after Edward died in battle. By then his own health was so far gone that he died within a year—not because he had no

choice but because he would not use his power to choose what was best for his life.

This graphic story illustrates that even though people know what is wrong in their lives, they may not change. Sheer knowledge is not enough. It also illustrates that people can feel very badly about their circumstances and still not change. Feeling badly is not enough. People must choose to change. James 2:12-20, although talking primarily about good works, emphasizes the importance of taking action:

> You will be judged on whether or not you are doing what Christ wants you to. So watch what you do and what you think; for there will be no mercy to those who have shown no mercy. But if you have been merciful, then God's mercy toward you will win out over his judgment against you.

> Dear brothers, what's the use of saying that you have faith and are Christians if you aren't proving it by helping others? Will that kind of faith save anyone? If you have a friend who is in need of food and clothing, and you say to him, "Well, good-bye and God bless you; stay warm and eat hearty," and then don't give him clothes or food, what good does that do?

> So you see, it isn't enough just to have faith. You must also do good to prove that you have it. Faith that doesn't show itself by good works is no faith at all—It is dead and useless.

> But someone may well argue, "You say the way to God is by faith alone, plus nothing; well, I say that good works are important too, for without good works you can't prove whether you have faith or not; but anyone can see that I have faith by the way I act."

> Are there still some among you who hold that "only believing" is enough? Believing in one God? Well, remember that the demons believe this too—so strongly that they tremble in terror! Fool! When will you ever learn that "believing" is useless without doing what God wants you to? Faith that does not result in good deeds is not real faith.

The point is that just thinking about something or talking about it is not enough. Even having strong feelings about an issue does not change the situation. We have to take action and put feet to our thoughts and feelings. Making a choice to change brings about health and freedom.

Raynald most likely protested verbally about his brother putting him in the dungeon. He probably thought about all of the freedom he lost. No longer could he go outside in the sunshine and enjoy the beauty of nature. He undoubtedly had emotions of fear, anger, anxiety, and depression at the turn of his circumstances. We can safely say that he might even have hated his brother. But none of his thoughts, emotions, or screaming gave him his freedom. He had the key to escape, but he did not use it. The name of the key was self-discipline.

Are you locked in a dungeon of emotional hurt and pain? Has the king of despair encircled you with walls of hopelessness? Would you like to experience freedom from anxiety and depression? Then do something! No steel bars are hindering your escape. You have just been fooled and blinded into thinking that there is no way out of your prison. Stop eating the pastries of self-pity. Stop gorging your mind with negative thoughts and fears about the future. Stop stuffing your hurts and losses into the enormous belly of feelings. Stop selecting self-abuse, self-doubt, and self-indulgence from the menu of thinking. Remove yourself from the table of torment. Instead, munch on self-control, self-determination, and self-sacrifice. Go on a diet of healthy thoughts. Feed on a positive attitude. Oh, it may not be easy…but the easy way won't build character and stamina.

Physical exercise is painful at first. The body fights against working on flabby and lazy muscles. You can think of all kinds of excuses not to go for a walk, ride your bicycle, or lift weights at a gym. But if you keep at the exercises long enough, you break through the barrier of discouragement. Soon you find enjoyment in exercise. You begin to have hope when you change from a couch potato, channel surfing your television set, to an individual with a sense of well-being. If you continue your exercises long enough, you form a habit and a lifestyle of healthy living. Most people seem to know this intellectually but fail to put it into practice in everyday experience.

The same is true in emotional well-being. We have to work out with new thoughts. We have to run in the circles of positive individuals. We have to break through the barriers of anxiety and depression and exercise the muscles of new thinking. Sometimes the process is a little messy and unpleasant, but if we don't give up too soon, the tunnel of dark and confused feelings will give way to the light of emotional health. We can develop the habit of a positive spirit, which can produce a lifestyle of inner peace.

Moaning and screaming about your pain is usually not the answer. I have found very few people who want to listen to my whimpering. Yet, to my surprise, I've occasionally discovered a few people who thought I was getting what I deserved. I think they were smiling at the sound of my lament. If I need compassion from others, I do well not to whine.

Experiencing a great sorrow is like entering a cave. We are overwhelmed by the darkness and loneliness. We feel that there is no escape from the prison-house of pain. But God in His loving kindness has placed on the invisible wall the lamp of faith, whose beams shall lead us back to the sunlit world, where work and friends and service await us.

HELEN KELLER

I'm reminded of the story of the man who was complaining about all of his problems. He moaned and groaned that the cross of trials he had to bear was too difficult.

"I would sure like to get rid of this cross," he said one day.

Zap! All of a sudden he was ushered into heaven and found himself standing before St. Peter. "What am I doing here?" he asked. "Did I die?"

"No," said St. Peter. "I just heard you complaining about your cross, and I thought I would help you out. Come with me to the warehouse of crosses. We'll see if we can find you a new one."

The man followed St. Peter to a large warehouse that was filled with crosses. There were big crosses and little crosses. There were crosses of all colors, shapes, and forms. Some of the crosses were made of glass and others of plastic. There was even a large cross on wheels.

St. Peter said, "You can go anywhere in the warehouse you like and select the cross of your choice."

The man began walking through the warehouse and looking at all the crosses. Hours later, he finally found one to his liking. It was a very small and light aluminum cross. He took it back to St. Peter for approval.

"A great choice," said St. Peter. "That's the very same cross you've been carrying."

Someone has said, "There is no such a thing as a problem that doesn't have a gift in it." Are you ready to discover that gift? What do you think you can learn from your anxiety and depression?

Dr. Karl Menninger, the famous psychiatrist who founded the Menninger Clinic, was asked one day how to prevent a nervous breakdown. He suggested that the best way would be to pull down all the shades in your house, turn off all the lights, lock all the doors, and "go across the railroad tracks and find someone in need and do something for him."

> If you want happiness for an hour—take a nap.
>
> If you want happiness for a day—go fishing.
>
> If you want happiness for a lifetime—help someone else.
>
> CHINESE PROVERB

We can easily become so focused on our own problems and trials that we don't see the needs of others around us. Often in our search for relief and contentment we forget that happiness is like a butterfly. If we try to catch the butterfly, it flies away. But when we busy ourselves with doing other tasks, the butterfly comes and lands on our shoulders. When we help others, we will find that our troubles disappear and delight lands in our life. The great Dr. Albert Schweitzer said, "One thing I know: The only ones among you who will be really happy are those who will have sought and found how to serve."

> There is one thing which gives radiance to everything. It is the idea of something around the corner.
>
> G.K. CHESTERTON

11

The RESCUED MIND
Understanding Suicide

⋄ ❖ ⋄

One of the bad things about depression is that it drains
us emotionally and makes us unable to handle
things that normally would not get us down.

BILLY GRAHAM

"BOB, I JUST DON'T CARE ANYMORE. I'm tired and can't handle the pressure. I hurt too much."

I was in my office preparing for my day of counseling when Echo telephoned. Her voice was very soft, and I could hardly understand what she was saying. As she kept talking, I could tell her speech was slow and slurred. I knew something was definitely wrong.

I asked Echo if she had taken any pills. She hesitated for a moment and then said yes and that "it doesn't matter anymore."

As I talked to Echo, I was snapping my fingers to get the attention of another counselor whose door happened to be open. I waved for him to come into the room. While she continued to talk, I wrote a note for him to call the emergency rescue team and send them to her house. I kept talking with Echo until she could no longer pronounce words. She hung up.

When I reached her home, the rescue team was bringing her out of the door on a stretcher. They immediately took her to the emergency room of the hospital and pumped her stomach. She survived her attempt at suicide.

The National Institute of Mental Health indicates that more than

30,000 people die by suicide in the United States each year. They also say that more than 90 percent of people who kill themselves have a diagnosable mental disorder, commonly a depressive disorder or a substance abuse disorder. The institute further informs us that suicide is the third-leading cause of death among 15- to 24-year-olds. The highest suicide rates in the U.S. are found in white men over age 85. Men are four times more likely to die from suicide than women…although women attempt suicide two to three times more often than men. Other sources estimate that there are 25 attempts of suicide for every death from suicide.

Further studies on suicide reveal the following information:

- Alcohol and drugs push depressed people toward suicide.

- Individuals with panic disorders have an increased risk of suicide.

- Adult men who have had same-sex relations are five times as likely to commit suicide as heterosexual men.

- Heavy-metal music and suicide share a strong tie.

- Obese women are 55 percent more likely to attempt suicide than women of normal weight.[1]

Clues Someone Is Contemplating Suicide

Often individuals contemplating suicide will give verbal clues of their intent. They may openly talk about suicide by asking for your opinion about it. Or they might ask for advice because they have a friend who is thinking about suicide. Questions like these are red flags.

Long-term depression and sleep problems may also be behavioral clues. Extreme guilt, shame, and embarrassment are other items to look for. Often feelings of hostility, revenge, tension, and anxiety are present. Suicidal individuals may give away possessions, update wills, increase insurance, and pay off long-standing debts. The clincher is when the individual has clearly thought-out plans coupled with access to things like guns, drugs, poison, and high-risk activities.

The above clues could be accompanied by the death of a loved one, a divorce, or separation. Loss of money, prestige, or a job may be factors. This includes retirement with no activities to take the place of the job. Sickness, serious illness, and disability could compound the picture. An estimated 75 percent of all who commit suicide have seen a physician within six months prior to their deaths. Accidents, injury, or prosecution for criminal offences could also be factors in suicide.

If you are personally having these experiences, or if you know someone who is, I strongly encourage you to seek advice and counsel. If you don't know anyone you can talk with, contact the National Hope Line Network. Their number is 1-800-Suicide (1-800-784-2433).

Dr. Maurice L. Farber, in his book *Theory of Suicide,* suggests the following thoughts with regard to the intention and outcome of suicide.

The individual wants to die and is *successful* in the suicide attempt.	The individual wants to die and is *unsuccessful* in the suicide attempt.
The individual does not want to die but does not get help and *dies*.	The individual does not want to die and *lives* through the attempted suicide because help comes.

If you are dealing with someone who is thinking about suicide, get as much information as possible to help you to determine how serious the person is.

SUICIDE RISK EVALUATOR

Name _____

Address_____

City _____ State _____ Zip _____

Home Phone_____ Work Phone _____

Friend or Relative Contact _____

Home Phone_____ Work Phone _____

Have you thought about suicide? ❑ yes ❑ no

How often do you have suicidal thoughts?

    ❑ never ❑ rarely ❑ increasingly

    ❑ frequently ❑ constantly

Have you ever attempted suicide before?

    ❑ yes ❑ no
    ❑ How many times _____
      Date of last time _____

What did you attempt to do? _____

_____

_____

_____

Did you talk with someone before your attempt?

    ❑ yes ❑ no

    Who was that individual? _____

Was your attempt at suicide ❑ spontaneous or was it
        ❑ planned?

Did you go to the hospital or see a doctor?

    Explain _____

_____

_____

How did you feel after the attempt?

    ❑ glad to be alive ❑ guilty
    ❑ sorry that you lived

Did an event trigger or cause your attempt? ❑ yes ❑ no

    Explain _____

_____

_____

_____

How would you describe your desire to live at this time?

❏ no desire to live ❏ moderate desire to live
❏ strong desire to live

Are you making plans now to commit suicide?

❏ yes ❏ no

Are you taking any drugs or alcohol at this time?

Drugs—what? _____

_____

Alcohol—how much? _____

_____

Do you see any hope in your future?

❏ yes ❏ no ❏ uncertain

If you were to give advice to people in a similar situation to yours, what would you say to them? _____

_____

_____

Are you willing to make a commitment to not harm yourself until you have talked to someone about your situation?

❏ yes ❏ no

It is important to take a person's comments seriously. Individuals who are seeking to help in this situation need to listen carefully to the person's feelings. They should be willing to discuss what is leading the person to have suicidal thoughts. They should not make any promises to keep secrets about this situation. It needs to be brought to the light of day, and family and friends should be informed so they can help the individual find hope.

Remove any items the individual could use to commit suicide. This includes guns, drugs, and poisons. Be loving but firm in your discussions.

Demonstrate that you care by establishing a no-suicide contract with the hurting individual. This has proven to be very important in many cases. However, don't rely solely on a verbal agreement and think that this will guarantee that the person will not commit suicide. A quarter of the people who agree to a suicide contract go on to commit suicide anyway. But the contract helps the suicidal person to realize that someone really cares and believes he or she can find hope.

The highest rate of suicide occurs in individuals who seem to be improving. The most likely time for the attempt to take place is six to eight months after they appear to be getting better. Those wishing to help would be wise to continually check on the individual for a year. Someone has suggested that suicide is a permanent solution for a temporary problem.

Suicide in the Bible

The Bible recounts several incidents of suicide. The motivation for these suicides varied. They included the escape of pain and torture, the desire for revenge, guilt and remorse, and sheer pride.

Abimelech was attempting to conquer a city with his army. As he and his men stormed a tower, a woman dropped a millstone on his head and cracked his skull. Talk about a migraine headache.

He immediately instructed his armor-bearer to pull out his sword and kill him. Because of his pride he said, "Draw your sword and kill me, so that they can't say 'A woman killed him'" (see Judges 9:50-54 niv).

Samson had been captured and blinded by the Philistines. They took him into the arena to make sport of him. As he stood between two pillars, he asked God to give him strength to inflict revenge and destruction on his enemies. He then pushed on the pillars, collapsing the building, and he and his enemies died (see Judges 16:28-30).

King Saul had been wounded by arrows in a battle and instructed his armor-bearer, "Draw your sword and run me through, or these uncircumcised fellows will come and run me through and abuse me." He wanted to escape torture and not give satisfaction to the Philistines. The armor-bearer would not kill the king, so Saul fell on his own sword and died. Seeing the king kill himself, the armor-bearer was terrified and also fell on his own sword and committed suicide (see 1 Samuel 31:1-6 niv).

Ahithophel instructed King David's son, Absalom, how and when to attack David in battle and kill him. Through certain events David got wind of the plot and began to pursue Ahithophel. When Ahithophel realized that his plan had failed and that David was after him, he rushed home, put his house in order, and hanged himself. He was fearful of retribution (see 2 Samuel 17:1-23).

Zimri was a captain in King Asa's army. He conspired against the king and killed him and ruled in his place. He then proceeded to exterminate a lot of other people. A man named Omri was commissioned by Israel to attack Zimri in the city of Tirzah. As the battle raged, Zimri realized that Omri would soon overrun the city. He fled to the citadel of the royal palace. Rather than face death by his enemies, Zimri set fire to the royal palace and died in the flames (see 1 Kings 16:9-19).

Judas Iscariot, one of the disciples of Jesus, betrayed Him for 30 pieces of silver. Shortly after the betrayal, Judas felt extreme guilt and remorse. He gave the money back to the chief priests and elders saying, "I have sinned in that I have betrayed innocent blood." Judas then went and hanged himself (see Matthew 27:3-5).

Strange Suicides

Suicides are sometimes strange. In high schools where a classmate has committed suicide, other young people may follow the person's example. Suicide almost appears to be contagious. We know it isn't an illness or disease that can be transmitted, but students with similar feelings seem to pick up some sort of psychological attraction. Perhaps they feel as if they have been given permission to die. Or perhaps they crave the same sort of attention the community lavished on someone else. Suicide can also be a warped form of punishment for those who are left behind.

Do you remember when you were a child and your feelings were hurt because you didn't get your way? You might have said to yourself, *You'll wish you were nice to me,* or *If I die, they'll feel bad for treating me this way.* Sometimes suicide is a deliberate way to hurt people.

Early Greek history includes the story of a town where a young girl committed suicide. Not long after, another girl committed suicide. A short time later several other girls followed their example. The leaders of the town were beside themselves trying to understand what was happening. Some thought the gods were punishing the town. Others were convinced evil spirits had cursed them. A few of the medical doctors thought a contagious mental illness was spreading. But no one could be sure what was causing the plague of suicide among the young women.

In desperation the doctors, educators, religious leaders, and political leaders came to a very old and wise man who lived in the town. They asked him, "What shall we do about this plague?"

He thought for a moment and then replied, "Make a proclamation and post it everywhere in the town. Be sure that everyone is aware of its contents." The leaders inquired as to what the proclamation should say.

The wise old man replied, "Write down this message for all to see: 'Be it known to all that the next young lady who commits suicide will have her body stripped naked. She then shall be carried through the town, and her naked body will be on display for everyone to see for three days in the town square. After that, her body will be buried.'"

An amazing thing happened. The plague stopped overnight, and no more suicides occurred. So much for mental illness. The point of the story is that suicide has a very strong psychological component. The person contemplating suicide has undoubtedly been hurt and suffered some loss—even simply the loss of prestige or reputation. The individual feels hopeless and helpless. An overwhelming sadness has darkened his or her spirit.

My grandfather on my father's side died when I was a young boy. I was too small to remember all of the details, but I do remember visiting him in his home in Denver. I recall him being bedridden with an illness. I stood by his bed and talked with him. A short time later, the family held a funeral service for him. No one talked about the details of his passing. Friends and neighbors assumed he passed away as a result of his illness. Not until later in life did I discover that he took his own life.

Apparently the illness was too much for him to bear. He wanted to escape the pain and suffering he was undergoing. This of course is understandable; many individuals in similar circumstances have had thoughts of escaping the trauma of what they are undergoing. Some people begin to believe they are a burden and their family would be better off without them. These depressive thoughts, when contemplated long enough, can lead many to end their lives.

The Grisly Side of Suicide

However, people who commit suicide do not often see another side of the picture. They don't understand how much of a mess they leave behind. The reason for this is that they are focused only on their needs, their pain, and their emotional despair. If you are thinking about suicide, my desire is not to hurt your feelings or make you feel bad. I don't intend to put you on a guilt trip but to help put you in touch with reality.

When people commit suicide they create a tremendous shock wave among the loved ones they leave behind. Grief overwhelms those who remain. They experience massive amounts of anger: anger with themselves for not being able to prevent the suicide and anger with the police, firemen, paramedics, doctors, ministers, and hospital personnel who were not able to rescue their loved ones in time. They have relatives who are upset with them. Often family and friends do not know how to react to a suicide, so they become silent and withdraw from the grieving family. Because of this separation and isolation, the mourning people sometimes have to develop new friendships.

Frequently those who are left behind struggle with funeral arrangements and loose ends of business dealings, legal documents, and creditors. The paperwork becomes a nightmare.

Those who are left behind can also struggle with physical ailments, sleeplessness, and possible suicidal thoughts themselves. They become filled with self-accusations, self-punishment, and guilt. Children who are left without a parent often become withdrawn, sullen, or openly delinquent in their behavior. The survivors' lives usually include years of turmoil just because the depressed individuals do not want to learn to face difficult issues and conquer them.

The people contemplating suicide may simply not care. They may take absolutely no responsibility for their actions or the welfare of their family. They may be consumed by thoughts about themselves.

I would do everything in my power to talk suicidal people out of their plans to kill themselves. I would try to get them immediate help. However, to be honest, I feel sorrier for the family they are destroying than I do for them.

Several years ago the wife of one of our acquaintances came home from work as usual. She noticed that her husband's car was in the driveway when she came in. She called out his name as she entered the door, but he didn't respond. She walked through the house looking for him but didn't see him. She glanced out into the backyard, but he was not there. She then figured he must be in the garage working on something.

She opened the door and was shocked to see him hanging from a garage rafter with a rope around his neck. At first, she couldn't process what she was seeing. Her husband was a practical joker, and she thought he was playing a prank on her.

She soon realized that this was not a practical joke. Her husband had committed suicide. She fell apart emotionally when she realized the truth.

That was the beginning of years of trying to put her life back together. She often woke up in the middle of the night, reliving the tragic event over and over again.

Just before Christmas, the son of one of my publishers committed suicide. His parents were beside themselves with grief. They were filled with unanswered questions. *Why couldn't we see this coming? Did we unknowingly contribute to his act of self-destruction? How could he do this to his family?*

Approximately ten days after I first wrote these thoughts about suicide, a relative of one of our staff members committed suicide. He had been troubled as a youth and disheartened as a man for quite a few years. He married young, and his marriage had been stormy. His depression became deeper as he turned to alcohol. In a moment of great despair he hanged himself.

Waking up in the middle of the night, his wife realized he wasn't in bed. She went looking for him and found him hanging in their carport. He left a devastated wife and a young son who had to grow up without a father. He also left relatives who had no concept of how to deal with the destruction he had created.

Any way you cut it, suicide creates a mess. Eggs have been broken, and they cannot be put back into their shells. The only thing we can attempt to do is to make an omelet out of the situation.

How much better to not break the eggs in the first place! My dear friend, if you are thinking about committing suicide, I implore you to get those thoughts out of your mind immediately. Burn up your suicide notes. Shake yourself back to the reality of the devastation you would create. Help is coming. A light is at the end of the tunnel. Hope is available for you. You cannot give up yet.

THE RACE
D. GROWBERG

"Quit, give up, you're beaten," they shout at me and plead,
"There's just too much against you now, this time you can't
    succeed."
And as I start to hang my head in front of failure's face,
My downward fall is broken by the memory of a race.
And hope refills my weakened will as I recall that scene,

For just the thought of that short race rejuvenates my being!
A children's race, young boys, young men, how I remember
      well.
Excitement, sure, but also fear. It wasn't hard to tell.

They all lined up, so full of hope, each thought to win that
      race
Or tie for first, or if not that, at least take second place.
And fathers watched from off the side, each cheering for his
      son,
And each boy hoped to show his dad that he would be the
      one!
The whistle blew and off they went, young hearts and hopes
      afire.
To win and be the hero there was each young boy's desire.
One boy in particular, whose dad was in the crowd,
Was running near the lead and thought, *My dad will be so
      proud.*

But as they speeded down the field, across a shallow dip,
The little boy, who thought to win, lost his step and slipped.
Trying hard to catch himself, his hands flew out to brace,
And mid the laughter of the crowd, he fell flat on his face.
So down he fell, and with him hope. He couldn't win it
      now.
Embarrassed, sad, he only wished to disappear somehow.
But as he fell, his dad stood up, and showed his anxious
      face,
Which to the boy so clearly said, *Get up and win the race.*

He quickly arose, no damage done, behind a bit, that's all.
He ran with all his mind and might to make up for his fall.
So anxious to restore himself, to catch up and to win,
His mind went faster than his legs…he slipped and fell
      again.
He wished then he'd quit before with only one disgrace.
"I'm hopeless as a runner now, I shouldn't try to race."
But in the laughing crowd he searched and found his
      father's face,
That steady look, which said again, *Get up and win the race.*

So up he jumped to try again ten yards behind the last.
If I'm to gain those yards, he thought, *I've got to move real
      fast!*
Exerting everything he had he regained eight or ten.
But trying so hard to catch the lead, he slipped and fell
      again.
Defeat! He lay there silently, a tear dropped from his eye.
*There's no sense running anymore, three strikes…I'm out…why
      try?*
The will to rise had disappeared, all hope had fled away.
So far behind, so error prone, a failure all the way.

I've lost. So what's the use? he thought. *I'll live with my dis-
      grace.*
But then he thought about his dad, who soon he'd have to
      face.
Get up! an echo shouted low, *Get up and take your place.*
You were not meant for failure here, get up and win the race!
With borrowed will, get up, it said. *You haven't lost at all.*
For winning is no more than this, to rise each time you fall!
So up he rose, to run once more, and with a new commit,
He resolved that, win or lose, at least he wouldn't quit.

So far behind the others now, the most he'd ever been,
Still he gave it all he had and ran as though to win.
Three times he'd fallen, stumbling, three times he'd rose
      again.
Too far behind to hope to win, he still ran to the end!
They cheered the winning runner as he crossed the line,
      first place.
Head high and proud and happy…no falling…no disgrace.
But when the fallen youngster had crossed that line, last
      place,
The crowd gave him the greater cheer for finishing the race.

And even though he came in last with head bowed low,
      unproud,
You would have thought he won that race, to listen to that
      crowd.
And to his dad he sadly said, "I didn't do so well."

"To me you won," his father said. "You rose each time you
    fell."
And now when things seem dark and hard and difficult to
    face,
The memory of that little boy helps me in my race.
For all of life is like that race, with ups and downs and all,
And all you have to do to win is rise each time you fall.

Quit, give up, you're beaten, they still shout in my face.
But deep within a voice still says, *Get up and win the race!*

12

The REVITALIZED MIND
The Importance of Rest and Relaxation

❖

What the will and reason are powerless to remove,
sleep melts like snow in water.

WALTER JOHN DE LA MARE

THE WAITER APPROACHED THE TABLE and started to speak, but I shook my head back and forth, indicating for him to remain silent. I could tell he was a little confused at first. His eyes quickly shifted from mine to the person sitting across the table from me. He then looked back at me, nodded slightly, and backed away from the table.

I had gone to lunch with a friend who was in his eighties. We had a tasty meal and were discussing a number of different topics while eating. At the close of the meal, he asked me a question. As I started to answer, I noticed him close his eyes momentarily. I paused for a few seconds, and he opened them. I continued to answer his question, but I could see his eyelids become heavy and close a second time. I continued talking for about another ten to fifteen seconds. Then I stopped. His eyes remained shut, and I could tell he was asleep. Shortly after this, the waiter approached the table, noticed what was happening, and departed.

As I sat there with my friend, I smiled to myself. He was not being rude to ask a question and then fall asleep. He was simply tired. I had mixed emotions. *Should I wake him up? That might not be polite, and he would probably be a little embarrassed. How long should I sit there and let him sleep?* I decided to remain silent and give him the rest he needed.

Almost ten minutes passed before he opened his eyes. As he did, I picked up the conversation where I had stopped as if there had been no interruption. My friend had no idea how long he'd been asleep, nor did I have any desire to make him feel uncomfortable by telling him what had happened.

It's been said that talking with yourself is okay, and answering yourself is okay, but when you disagree with your answers, you may have a problem. Well, Geraldo had a problem. His behavior had been strange for several days. He was at first very edgy and irritable. Then he began to carry on conversations with himself. Eventually he began to have mild hallucinations and believe he heard voices.

Geraldo was in his junior year at the university. During the day he went to school, and in the evenings he held a job as a waiter to help pay his tuition fees. After work, he stayed up late studying for his finals. This had been going on for more than a week. He had been living on caffeine and junk food and had virtually gone without sleep. His extremely stressful schedule had pushed his body, his thinking capacity, and his emotional resiliency to the limits. He was close to a breaking point.

According to the National Sleep Foundation, more than 74 million American adults suffer from some form of sleep loss. They have trouble getting to sleep, sleep restlessly, wake up too early, or sleep very little a few nights a week or more. Thirty-nine percent of those surveyed get less than seven hours a night. In addition, 37 percent indicated that their lack of sleep made them drowsy during the day and interfered with their work or activities. Sleep difficulties generate more than $70 billion a year in business for drug companies. Hardly a day will pass that you will not be aware of the advertising of some form of sleep medication on television, in the newspaper, in magazines, or on billboards.

The National Highway Traffic Safety Administration estimates that more than 100,000 traffic accidents are related to fatigue and drowsiness each year. These accidents have caused more than 1500 deaths, tens of thousands of injuries, and many lasting disabilities. The estimated financial cost of the reduced productivity and property damage caused by these accidents is in the billions of dollars.

Our counseling center's intake sheet included this question:

What is your sleep pattern like?

❏ restful   ❏ restless   ❏ little sleep   ❏ too much sleep

A change in sleep patterns, a lack of sleep, or too much sleep can be strong indicators of anxiety and depression. As in the case of Geraldo, extreme stress and sleep loss have been known to generate hallucinations.

Sleep loss has been tied not only to anxiety, depression, hallucinations, and motor vehicle accidents but also to...

- increased appetite and greater likelihood of obesity
- increased risk of diabetes due to the body's impairment of the use of insulin
- increased risk of hypertension and cardiovascular problems
- increased likelihood of alcohol and drug abuse
- lack of ability to concentrate and pay attention

Insomnia and sleep-related problems have many causes. Any of these items, alone or combined with others, can disrupt sleep:

- Accidents, injuries, and the accompanying pain
- Aging, menopause, and chronic illness and/or disease
- Alcohol
- Alzheimer's
- Anger, bitterness, thoughts of revenge, and an unforgiving spirit
- Career changes
- Changes in the weather
- Diet—eating meals too close to bedtime (less than three hours before bed) and ingesting caffeine
- Divorce and separation
- Family pressures and concerns involving children
- Financial worries
- Gastrointestinal problems, including heartburn
- Grief and various types of hurts and losses
- Narcolepsy
- Nicotine

- Nightmares and bad dreams
- Poor sleep habits
- Pregnancy
- Prostate difficulties and frequent urination
- Relationship dysfunctions
- Restless leg syndrome
- School and part-time work
- Shift work
- Sleep environment—too much noise, too much light, too much heat, poor mattress, or a poor pillow
- Sleep terrors in children
- Sleeping in a different environment
- Snoring or sleep apnea
- Substance abuse and the taking of certain medications
- Traveling and jet lag
- Work pressures, layoffs, and retirement

Many individuals who suffer from sleep disturbances share similar emotional characteristics. They have a tendency to worry about how they will respond to future relationships, circumstances, and dreams. They have obsessive thoughts that tend to be pessimistic and negative. They have depressive thoughts that replay past hurts over and over again. They dwell on past failures and regrets. Their outlook tends to be catastrophic, and they often envision the worst possible outcome. They seem to be overwhelmed by their inability to control their anxious thoughts. All of these characteristics give rise to insomnia and restless sleep.

Parnell turned five years old, and his parents took him to Disneyland for his birthday. The day started early so the family could drive three hours just to get to Disneyland. Everything went well for most of the day. Late in the afternoon, Parnell began to act up. He became a little whiny and irritable. His parents thought he might be hungry, so they all stopped for a bite to eat. That did help the situation for a little while, but about two hours later he began to whine again. The whining soon became belligerence, which shortly turned into a full-blown temper tantrum.

His parents were worn out and were becoming exasperated. They both looked at him and agreed. "I think Parnell is tired and needs to go to bed and get some sleep." When Parnell heard their words, he really fell apart. He didn't want to leave Disneyland, and he surely didn't want to go to bed.

Can you remember when you were a child and were having a bad day? Did you hate hearing the adults around you say you needed to go to bed? Did you fight their conclusion just as Parnell did? And yet the whole world looked different the next morning even if you cried yourself to sleep the night before.

Could the same be true for adults? Maybe what some people need more than anything else is sleep. Sleep is a great healer of many physical ailments and many emotional difficulties. Hurts, fears, anxieties, and depressions have a tendency to melt away as one gets needed rest. But just like little children, adults are reluctant to admit that what they need more than anything else is sleep.

The Bible contains an interesting story that illustrates this point. First Kings 17–19 recounts a story about Elijah the prophet. As you might recall, Elijah went before King Ahab and informed him that no rain would fall for three and a half years.

As soon as Elijah made his proclamation to the king, he fled and hid himself. For most of the next three and a half years, Elijah kept in hiding because he was a wanted man. Everyone in Samaria experienced a severe famine, and they blamed Elijah for the problem. He was lonely, rejected, and under the stress of running for his life.

To add to his stress, God instructed him to stand again before King Ahab, whose anger had been building for more than three years. Elijah takes on not only the wrath of Ahab and the people of the land but also a showdown with 450 prophets of Baal and 400 prophets of Asherah. (The 400 prophets of Asherah were Queen Jezebel's special prophets.)

The confrontation took place on Mount Carmel. Elijah stands before King Ahab, the children of Israel, and the 850 prophets and makes a statement. He challenges everyone there to choose to follow Baal or to follow God. Both sides build altars and agree that if Baal brings fire out of the sky to light the altar, the people will follow Baal, and if God sends fire to light the altar, the people will follow God. As you will recall, God and not Baal sends fire from the sky. The prophets of Baal and Asherah are then slain, and the people agree to follow God.

The next day, Jezebel sends a message to Elijah that she is going to have him killed. He runs for his life into the wilderness in deep depression and wants to die. He says, "It is enough! Now, LORD, take my life, for I am no better than my fathers!" (1 Kings 19:4 NKJV). Elijah had come to the end of his string. In deep despair, he was ready to throw in the towel and give up. Let's look at the buildup of stress in Elijah's life:

- He made a proclamation that there would be no rain.
- He ran and hid for three and a half years.
- Nobody liked him.
- His reputation was destroyed.
- People said bad things about him.
- He had an emotional face-off with Ahab.
- He challenged the 850 prophets.
- He stood alone before the children of Israel.
- He had a great victory.
- He had to personally walk down the mountain and slay the 850 prophets. (I can hardly picture that.)
- He then climbed back up the mountain to wait for rain.
- As the rain started to come, Elijah ran ahead of Ahab's chariot back to the city. (It was not a short run—it was more than 20 miles.)
- The next day, Jezebel threatens to kill Elijah.
- Nothing has changed. Elijah is still a hunted man. He flees a day's journey into the wilderness, running for his life.
- At this point, the stress buildup of more than three years is too great. The final straw has broken his emotional back, and he asks God if he might die.

Hello! No wonder Elijah is anxious and depressed. He is a physical and emotional wreck. He collapses under a juniper tree and falls into an exhausted sleep. After a while an angel touches him and tells him to get up and eat. After he has eaten, he lies down and again falls into a much-needed sleep.

Have you been having a long buildup of problems and difficulties? Are you feeling tired and alone? Are you angry at the unfairness and injustice you face? Have you experienced loss, broken relationships, and unresolved conflict with others? Are you feeling a little sorry for yourself? Are you feeling depressed? Has this been going on for a long time? Would you like a way out? Would you like some relief?

May I have permission to suggest, as Parnell's parents did, that bedtime has come? A good solid base of sleep is an important starting point for getting a fresh perspective and renewed energy. Don't fight it the way Parnell did. Instead, collapse under a tree like Elijah. Or better yet, on a nice soft bed.

Fighting Insomnia and Getting a Better Sleep

Sleep requirements vary according to age. Babies and younger children may need nine to eleven hours of sleep. Teenagers do better on nine or ten hours of sleep. Studies seem to indicate that at least seven hours help us to give our optimal best. Those who are older sometimes get far less than seven hours, but they often have cat naps during the day to help make up the seven hours they need. Of course, you can operate on fewer hours, but it takes a physical and emotional toll as sleep debt builds up.

The body seems to operate on sleep cycles and rhythms. These rhythms last about 90 minutes. When you fall asleep, you enter a NREM (non-rapid eye movement) sleep. This is a light sleep where we begin to disengage with our environment. Our breathing and heart rate become regular. Our body temperature goes down a little.

After about 90 minutes we begin to move into the deepest and most restorative sleep. It is called REM (rapid eye movement) sleep. During REM sleep our brain is active. We dream, and our eyes dart back and forth under our closed eyelids. Our muscles become very relaxed. Our breathing and heart rate can become irregular. REM sleep constitutes about 25 percent of the sleep time, and NREM sleep makes up the other 75 percent.

Here are a few ways you can improve your sleep habits:

- Avoid napping during the day. You may not be tired when you go to bed at your regular time.

- Get a comfortable mattress. Endeavor to purchase a mattress that is not lumpy or one in which you feel the springs poke certain parts of your body. Also choose a pillow that best serves your needs. Mattresses usually last nine or ten years.

- Maintain a cool temperature. Cool sleeping conditions make for a more restful sleep. Benjamin Franklin addressed this concept in the 1700s:

    When you are awakened by this uneasiness, and find you cannot easily sleep again, get out of bed, beat up and turn your pillow, shake the bedclothes well, with at least twenty shakes, then throw the bed open and leave it to cool; in the meanwhile, continuing undressed, walk about your chamber till your skin has had time to discharge its load, which it will do sooner as the air may be dried and colder. When you begin to feel the cold air unpleasant, then return to your bed, and you will soon fall asleep, and your sleep will be sweet and pleasant.

- Keep your bedroom dark. The darkness will help to encourage sleep. Blackout curtains and eye shades may help.

- Don't exercise within three hours of going to bed. Exercising has a stimulating effect on the body, not a relaxing effect.

- Avoid caffeine before bed. Caffeine is a stimulant. This includes coffee, tea, soft drinks, and chocolate. Avoid alcohol and nicotine as well.

- Move your clock. If you wake up during the night and see the time, you might remain awake, worrying that you won't wake up on time.

- Eliminate as much noise as possible. Strange sounds can wake you up out of your much-needed sleep. Some people find ear plugs helpful. Others like the white noise of fans or humidifiers.

- Place a paper and pen by your bed. Often when we go to bed we think about something we must do the next day. We keep rolling it over and over in our mind to make sure we will remember it when we wake up in the morning. Instead of lying awake and trying to lock it into your memory, write it down. That way you can relax, knowing that you won't forget it for the next day. Also, if you wake up during the night and have a thought or two, write them down. Tell yourself you will think about them in the morning when you're not so tired.

- Try not to make your bedroom a place for work, hobbies, eating meals, paying bills, resolving conflicts, engaging in competitive games, or writing letters. All of these activities tend to stimulate rather than relax, especially if they remind you of all the things you need to do or the things you haven't completed. Keep your bedroom for making love and for sleeping.

- Establish a regular and relaxing bedtime routine. It could include listening to soothing music, reading a book, soaking in a hot bath, and utilizing breathing techniques and relaxation methods.

- Some children encounter sleep terrors. This is a shock to the parents. The children may have their eyes wide open and seem to be awake when really they are sound asleep and are experiencing some extreme fear. You can find suggestions for dealing with sleep terrors on the Internet.

- If you snore or your mate snores, you don't have to suffer through it. There are many ways to help eliminate snoring. Avail yourself of them. If you or your partner suffers from sleep apnea, consult an ear, nose, and throat specialist.

- Some individuals suffer from urinary urgency caused by an enlarged prostate or other problems. If this is the case, be sure to contact a physician to be checked out. Some medications can help in this situation.

If you cannot fall asleep within 20 minutes, or you wake during the night and cannot go back to sleep within 20 minutes, get up. Go into another room and engage in some relaxing activity, such as reading or listening to music. If that does not seem to lead to sleep, do some tasks you have been putting off, such as polishing your shoes, cleaning a closet, paying bills, straightening a bookshelf, organizing business records, or doing a hobby. You will feel some satisfaction that you have accomplished something positive rather than just lying there fretting over the fact that you can't fall asleep.

Deep Breathing

If you want to die, all you have to do is stop breathing. We all know this instinctively, and the majority of us do not want to die, so we breathe in and out. But most of this breathing is unconscious. It becomes conscious when we are underwater and our lungs are about to burst. We fight and struggle to the surface of the water, attempting to gasp the life-giving air we so desperately need.

You breathe approximately 23,000 times a day. When you are anxious and depressed, you have a tendency to take shallow breaths. Unless we are in some form of emergency or we are working out, breathing deeply takes a conscious effort. It doesn't come naturally.

When most people start to cry, their muscles tighten, and shallow breathing occurs. If you want to help to keep yourself from crying, deep breathing helps. It relaxes muscles all over your body.

Deep breathing can help to relieve muscle tension created by anxiety and depression. It also helps to reduce anger and fear. Deep breathing can be a very helpful tool when we find ourselves in difficult situations and also when we want to relax and go to sleep at night.

To practice deep breathing, lie down on the floor or a bed. Draw your knees up and allow them to spread apart slightly. Begin to relax and breathe deeply. Slowly draw in your breath to the count of six. Hold your breath for the count of six. Then slowly let your breath out to the count of six.

To learn to breathe deeply, lie on the floor and place a book on your stomach. As you breathe in, your abdominal muscles should lift the book. As you breathe out, the book will fall with the lowering of your stomach. If you want to practice breathing deeply while sitting up, place both of your hands on your stomach and slowly breathe in and out to the count of six as if you were lying on the floor. By having your hands on your stomach, you can feel if you are breathing deeply.

To have a good exchange of air while you are walking, change your count a little. To breathe in, take in four short breaths in a row. Don't hold your breath. Immediately after drawing in the fourth breath, exhale with four short separate exhales.

If you are running and want a good exchange of air, change your breathing count to two. Two quick separate inhales, followed by two quick separate exhales. The breathing in and out to the count of two will give you sufficient air while you are running and will help you to run longer distance. Counting to two—in and out—will help you to concentrate on your breathing rather than your running. You won't run very far if your system is out of oxygen.

Conversely, when you are under stress or your emotions are running high, endeavor to control your breathing. Breathe deeply. It will assist you to face difficult situations, relax muscles that are tightening, and focus on control. If you can learn to control your breathing, you can also learn to control your emotions. Give it a try. You'll be surprised.

Relaxation

To wind down during the day or before you go to bed at night, try the following exercise. Ideally, find a quiet room where you can turn down the lights and play soft music. However, you can do the same exercises without the dim lights and soft music. The length of time can vary from ten to twenty minutes.

1. Lie on the floor on your back.
2. Place a pillow under your neck, filling the gap that is normally created when lying down.
3. Place a pillow under your knees. Rest your arms comfortably at your sides.
4. Close your eyes and begin to slowly breathe in and out. Breathe in to the count of six. Hold your breath for the count of six. Let out your breath to the count of six. With each breath in, energy enters the body. With each breath out, tension leaves the body. Concentrate on breathing in and out for about 20 exhales.
5. Next, make a fist and tightly squeeze each hand. Hold the fist for a count of six. Then spread out your fingers as far as you can to the count of six. Do that three times and then relax your hands entirely.
6. Next, contract your arm muscles to the count of six and then relax them as you did with your hands. Tighten your arms three times and then relax.
7. Next, contract both of your legs in the same way you

tightened your arms. Hold the tension for a count of six and then relax. Do it three times.

8. Next, contract and relax your stomach muscles in a similar fashion.

9. Next, contract and relax your chest muscles in a similar fashion.

10. Next, contract and relax your shoulder muscles in a similar fashion.

11. Next, contract and relax your neck muscles in a similar fashion.

12. Finally, contract and relax your face and head muscles in a similar fashion.

13. When you are finished contracting and relaxing muscles, let your entire body relax. Concentrate on breathing in and out normally, not keeping a six count. Energy comes in on the inhale, and tension goes out on the exhale.

14. Now, begin to imagine your favorite spot. It could be at the beach or in the mountains. You may prefer relaxing on an island getaway or floating in a hot-air balloon. Visualize the spot in your mind. You may want to feel the warmth of the sun on your body or the coolness of water. It is up to you. Whichever spot you select, begin to visualize what you see in detail. What sounds would you like to hear? What smells would you like to smell? What would you like to feel? Imagine these things, and continue to relax deeper with each breath.

15. Determine how much time you have to spend in relaxation before you begin the exercise. If you have 15 minutes, ask your body to remind you when it is time to get up. Our bodies have an amazing ability to keep very accurate time. When the time comes to end your relaxation and visualization period, take ten last relaxing breaths and then get up. You will be amazed at how refreshed you will feel.

Relaxation can also take on other forms:

- going to a movie
- reading a book

- talking with friends
- listening to music
- taking a leisurely walk
- going on a picnic
- soaking in a hot tub or a warm bath
- playing sports
- sitting in the sun
- taking a nap
- being quiet and meditating alone
- reading the Bible
- writing to family and friends

Part of the reason breathing and tension-releasing exercises are helpful is that you can't be anxious and relax at the same time. Worry cannot prevent fire, flood, drunk drivers, tornados, earthquakes, hurricanes, burglary, robbery, murder, flat tires, traffic jams, roadwork, or detours. If you have been struggling with concern, worry, anxiety, and flat-out fear, has it helped you in any way? My guess is that it hasn't.

Maybe it's time to let go of the need to predict, protect, and preserve. Maybe it's important to realize that worry and anxiety are simply that… they are worry and anxiety and not reality. Reality comes from what we can touch, hear, smell, taste, and see, not from what we imagine or fear.

Exercise

A number of years ago I received a phone call from a pastor of a medium-sized church. He shared with me some of the frustrations, fears, and problems he was facing with his congregation. A recent elders' meeting had left him saddened, hurt, angry, and depressed. Things had been said about him that were untrue, and he was unable to defend himself or correct the gossip. He was thinking about quitting and giving up the ministry.

I listened to his story and made several suggestions. The first suggestion I made was that he needed to join a gym and start working out as soon as he could. I told him that much of what he was feeling would disappear as exercise cleared his thinking.

After several weeks I received a second phone call. The pastor sounded

> The only exercise some people get is jumping to conclusions, running down their friends, sidestepping responsibility, dodging issues, passing the buck, and pushing their luck.

like a different man. He was more upbeat and not depressed. He still had some difficulties to deal with at the church, but he now had a new attitude about those problems. He is still in the ministry.

In a 1999 study of fifty-six severely depressed people at Duke University, scientists found that three 30-minute workouts each week brought relief equal to drug treatment. A Psychometric Medicine study found that 40 percent of patients relying on drugs were stricken with depression again within six months versus only 8 percent who exercised.[1]

Over 1,000 studies have been done on the benefits of exercise in relieving depression. Although it is not certain that exercise can prevent depression, it certainly plays an enormous factor in overcoming depressive thinking.[2]

A comprehensive analysis of 80 of these studies revealed that, overall, depression scores decreased by approximately half in the exercise groups. This finding applied across all age and gender lines, and the longer participants stayed with a program of regular exercise, the better they felt.[3]

Physical exercise is beneficial because it helps to reduce excessive adrenaline in the body. Adrenaline is a strong component in anxiety and various forms of arousal. Exercise also helps by increasing the body's production of endorphins. Endorphins are our bodies' own form of morphine. They help to reduce pain and seem to create an overall sense of well-being. Exercise is a way to release emotional frustrations and relax our muscles.

Here are a few of the great benefits of exercise:

- boosts self-esteem
- burns calories
- creates a sense of balance
- decreases anxiety

- dispels depression
- encourages mental sharpness
- enhances appetite
- hardens muscles
- heightens sexual interest
- helps establish self-discipline
- helps prevent constipation
- helps stabilize diabetes
- helps with low back pain
- helps you feel stronger
- helps you feel younger
- improves cardiovascular function
- improves lung function
- improves sleep
- improves stamina
- increases flexibility
- increases self-respect
- increases your ability to handle stress
- loosens stiff joints
- provides opportunities to meet new friends
- reduces chronic pain
- reduces fatigue
- speeds metabolism
- stimulates digestion
- strengthens bones and stimulates bone growth
- strengthens stomach and back

Exercise can take many different forms, such as weight lifting, brisk walking, bicycling, running, swimming, or competing in various other sports. Many exercise programs can be done at home. Many gyms are open 24 hours a day to accommodate those who have staggered working schedules.

If you are experiencing anxiety and depression, become involved with programs that have trainers and coaches. Or join with others in group activities. This provides encouragement and accountability to start and continue an exercise program.

The person who does not find time for exercise may have to find time for illness.

13

The RECLAIMED MIND

The Power of Positive Self Talk

❖ ❖ ❖

*You are today where your thoughts
have brought you; you will be tomorrow where
your thoughts take you.*

JAMES ALLEN

"MY HUSBAND MAY LEAVE ME," Heather said as she plopped down on the couch and sighed. She was wearing gray sweats that hadn't seen a washing for quite some time. Her hair looked a little disorganized, and one of her tennis shoes was unlaced. She looked sad, depressed, and discouraged.

"I think he's mad at me," she continued. "I don't think his mother likes me either. She's such a perfectionist, and I certainly don't fit her mold." I noticed the anger in her comment.

Heather had her hand in front of her mouth, and she was looking down. I was quiet as she paused, deep in thought. I glanced at the intake questionnaire and noticed she'd checked the box indicating that she was sleeping more than ten hours a day.

I spoke. "Heather, could you help me understand why you think your husband might want to leave you?"

She slowly lifted her eyes toward mine. "I think he thinks I'm a lazy slob."

Again I sensed a tinge of anger even though she continued with a saddened facial expression. "I think his mother thinks that too."

There's that tone again, I thought. "What has led you to that conclusion?"

"He always complains that the house is a mess."

"Is it?" That question took her a little off guard.

I followed with another question before she could answer. "Are you a slob?"

She hesitated for a moment, pursed her lips slightly, and nodded her head up and down.

"If your husband thinks your house is messy and you think it's messy, why don't you clean it up?"

She sighed and shook her head back and forth. "I'm too depressed, and I don't have any energy. I don't feel like doing anything around the house. I just turn on the TV and vegetate on the couch."

"When evening comes and you haven't done anything all day, how do you feel?"

"Guilty and angry."

"Guilty?"

"Yes. Guilty because I know I should do something about cleaning our home, but I just sit there. Then I feel angry at myself for not doing any work around the house. That makes me more depressed, and then I start to eat junk food."

We talked for a while longer, and then I asked, "Would you like to feel better?"

"Yes, of course." She was now looking at me quizzically.

"Well, I think you'd feel a great deal better if you'd clean your house."

"I just don't have the energy. It's too big of a job."

"How do you eat an elephant?" I asked.

She was now looking at me as if I had lost my mind. "I don't know."

"One bite at a time. Let's begin to eat the elephant of your messy house one bite at a time. Let's break it down to smaller pieces. How about starting with cleaning your bedroom?"

Now both of her hands went up. "It's too big of a mess."

"How big is your bedroom?"

"What do you mean?"

"What is the size of your bedroom? Most bedrooms are about twelve by fourteen."

"I guess ours is a little larger."

"Say, fourteen by sixteen?"

"Probably."

"How long would it take you to clean up a fourteen by sixteen space?"

"I don't know…it's a big mess."

"Could you clean it in a half a day?"

"You don't understand."

I ignored her statement. "Could you clean it up in three hours?"

"You don't seem to get it. I'm depressed, and I don't have any energy."

I continued. "What if I gave you five hundred dollars? Could you clean it in three hours?"

Heather shook her head back and forth.

"Okay, what if I gave you a thousand dollars to clean it in two hours? Could you clean up your bedroom?"

"You're not listening," she said.

"All right," I said. "What if I gave you ten thousand dollars to clean up the room in two hours?" She started to respond but I broke in, "This is my final offer…what if I gave you fifty thousand? Could you clean up a fourteen by sixteen room in an hour?"

She had a frustrated look on her face.

"All right, what's your price?" I said.

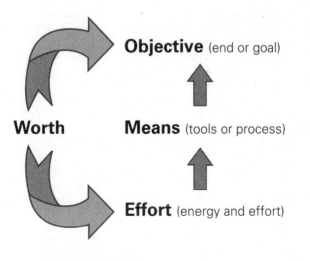

The point of the exercise was to illustrate the fact that we do what we want to do in life because we get something out of it. Heather was getting something by not cleaning her house. She was getting attention. (It was mostly negative attention from her husband and mother-in-law.) She was also getting out of a task she didn't like to do and was excusing or blaming it on her depression…in spite of the fact that she admitted she was sloppy. What would make Heather begin to clean up her house?

She needed a reward. The reward of not losing her husband would help her to put forth the effort to clean the house. We only change our behavior and our thinking if we hurt enough or the goal is something we really desire. Otherwise, why change at all?

Let's review for a moment. What brings about anxiety or depression? Is it caused by medication? In rare cases it can be. Is it caused by the weather? Not directly. Two people can live in the same location, and one will be happy and the other depressed. Is it caused by an accident or an illness? That's possible, but it's rare. Is it caused by a chemical imbalance? Not usually. Chemical imbalances are more likely to be the results of emotions and not the cause of them.

The primary causes of anxiety and depression are our thinking process and our reaction to stress and overload. Emotional difficulties usually occur because of our perception of life events, conflicted interpersonal relationships, and personal dissatisfaction.

Sometimes we are the instigators or primary causes of our own fears and angers. At other times we are innocent victims of circumstances outside of our control. Perhaps we are laid off from work, our house burns down, or a drunk driver kills one of our family members. Life is filled with many different forms of hurts and losses.

- Real losses can include financial problems, death, illness, and accidents.

- Abstract losses have to do with things like love, reputation, being needed, and self-respect.

- Imagined losses can include things like envy, jealousy, and suspicion.

- Threatened losses can include things like a lawsuit, a robbery, or an assault.

In either case, whether we are the cause or the victim, our perception of what is happening to us is what creates the anxiety and gives rise to our depression. The bottom line is that we are not always responsible for what happens to us, but we are responsible for our thoughts and attitudes about what is going on in our lives.

> Worry never climbed a hill,
> Worry never paid a bill,
> Worry never dried a tear,
> Worry never calmed a fear,
> Worry never darned a heel,
> Worry never cooked a meal,
> It never led a horse to water,
> Nor ever did a thing it "oughter."

Now granted, zeroing in on the positive rather than the negative is not an easy task. It's plain hard work and requires focus and a whole lot of intestinal fortitude. As a rule of thumb, focusing on ourselves often leads to anxiety and depression. When we think of others, our anxiety and depression are more likely to go away. Our depression lifts when we involve ourselves in some task, be it work, exercise, or lifting the spirits of other people.

I never met a person, I don't care what his condition, in whom I could not see possibilities. I don't care how much a man may consider himself a failure, I believe in him, for he can change the thing that is wrong in his life any time he is ready and prepared to do it. Whenever he develops the desire, he can take away from his life the thing that is defeating it. The capacity for reformation and change lies within.

PRESTON BRADLEY

If anxiety and depression arise out of our thinking and perception of life events, how can we change our perceptions? That is a question of extreme importance.

To begin, we need to understand that we frequently create **A**utomatic **N**egative **T**houghts in our minds. Daniel G. Amen in his book *Healing Anxiety and Depression* calls these thoughts mental **ANTs.**

Listed below are some of the ANTs that crawl about in our minds and eat away positive thinking.

absolutely	constantly	everything	no way
all	continually	forever	nonstop
always	endless	impossible	perpetually
ceaselessly	every time	incessantly	unceasingly
completely	everyone	never	unchangeable

It is very easy to develop a black-and-white, all-or-nothing thinking process. It may include strong messages of what we should have done, could have done, must do, or ought to do. Catastrophic perceptions like these often lead us to make unfair comparisons and personalizations that relate everything to us. Then we begin to overgeneralize and give ourselves negative labels.

a nobody	dope	hopeless	ninny
bad	dreadful	idiot	nincompoop
blockhead	dumbbell	impotent	nitwit
buffoon	failure	inadequate	pathetic
chump	fool	jerk	pig
clown	freak	loser	powerless
despicable	goof	lunatic	stupid
ding-a-ling	half-wit	monster	undeserving
dingbat	helpless	moron	

Sometimes we call ourselves names, and sometimes other people make fun of us. Do you remember the little children's singsong? "Sticks and stones may break my bones but names will never hurt me." Well, the truth is that name-calling does hurt us whether we do it to ourselves or other people do it to us. If you want to move away from anxiety and depression, begin to stomp on the ANTs of cataclysmic words and negative labeling.

You can begin to do this by challenging your thoughts. When you begin to think, *Nobody likes me, and everyone thinks I'm stupid,* challenge

The Potential Unhealthiness of Self-Talk

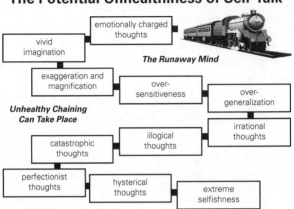

that thought. With more than 7 billion people on the planet, surely we could find some people who would like you. And honestly, could *everyone* possibly think you're stupid? Thoughts like these probably aren't based on reality.

You are much more likely to be reacting emotionally to a damaged relationship with someone of importance in your life. You could be frustrated and hurt over the situation and not know how to change it.

I'm reminded of the story of one young man who wanted to get rid of his anxiety and depression. He traveled all over the world talking with counselors, psychologists, psychiatrists, and very wise people. One day he heard of an extremely perceptive old man named Telamon who lived high in the mountains of Tibet.

After many days of travel, the young man came upon Telamon's wooden cabin. He took a deep breath and knocked on the old man's door. It opened and there stood a short man with a wrinkled face and a long gray beard. The young man introduced himself and asked the old man if he was Telamon. The old man carefully looked at the young man and said, "Perhaps."

For several days the young man told of his struggle with anxious thoughts and depressive moods. He recounted past hurts and expressed his future fears. The old man listened politely and quietly. Finally the young man ran out of things to say. He sat for a moment and then asked Telamon, "Do you have any wise thoughts for me?"

The old man said, "Perhaps." He then motioned for the young man to follow him. They walked down a winding path toward a beautiful lake.

Upon arriving the young man said, "This is breathtaking. Is this where I will find the answer?"

"Perhaps," replied the old man.

Telamon took the young man to the side of the lake and said, "Get on your knees. Bend over and look carefully into the water." The young man followed his instructions. He could see his own face in the reflection of the still water. He was wondering if the lake contained some special magic.

Suddenly, the old man pushed the young man's head underwater. He struggled desperately to break free but could not. The old man's grip was very strong. Soon he could feel himself starting to lose consciousness from the lack of air.

At that point, the old man pulled the young man's head out of the water. The young man gasped for air and yelled, "What are you doing? You almost killed me! Are you crazy?"

"Perhaps," said the old man. "But when you truly search for the way to overcome anxiety and depression as you were fighting for air, you will become wise."

As you struggle to overcome anxiety and depression, are you willing to make the necessary adjustments, or like the young man, do you just want to tell your story of misery?

Let me share with you a few random thoughts about anxiety, depression, and the task of reclaiming your mind. In the next chapters we will proceed to what I believe will be the secret that will set you free from hopelessness and despair, but here are some techniques that will help you get rid of the ANTs.

Stop!

Yell out loud, "STOP! STOP! STOP!" The shock of hearing your own voice will help to change your thinking pattern. Then say out loud (with gusto) "Think new thoughts! Think new thoughts! Think new thoughts!" This thought-stopping process can help to break the chain of cataclysmic words and negative labeling. We have to learn to put up a fight against the thoughts that pull us down emotionally. We need to flee from disruptive thinking.

After you shock yourself and break the negative thinking pattern, replace the disruptive thinking with positive thoughts. Begin to list (out loud) all the things you can be thankful for. Of course, you may not always be in a place where you can use this technique. Sitting in the middle of a meeting and shouting out loud to yourself may strike those around you as quite strange. You may have to do the same exercise in the quietness of your own mind.

> Count your blessings, not your crosses,
> Count your gains, not your losses.
> Count your joys instead of your woes,
> Count your friends instead of your foes.
> Count your health, not your wealth.

James, the brother of Jesus, suggested something similar to this when he wrote about resolving conflict and the devil's influence on our thinking. "Submit yourselves, then, to God. Resist the devil, and he will flee from you. Come near to God and he will come near you" (James 4:7-8 NIV).

The apostle Paul encourages us to live a life of thanksgiving: "Be joyful always; pray continually; give thanks in all circumstances, for this is God's will for you in Christ Jesus" (1 Thessalonians 5:16-18 NIV).

Distraction

Grab an ice cube out of the freezer and hold it tightly in your hand. The physical act of getting the ice cube and holding it will help short-circuit your negative thinking. The coldness and the melting water will distract you from your cataclysmic thoughts.

Or get a large rubber band and put it on your wrist. Find one that does not fit tight, but dangles loosely. When negative thoughts begin to come, pull the rubber band away from the inside of your wrist and let it go. Do that a couple of times, and I guarantee it will help to change your negative thinking process and anxiety about the future. You'll stop giving in to unproductive thoughts just to avoid the pain!

This will not cure your anxiety and depression. It only helps to change what you are thinking about. When you change your thinking, your feelings begin to change. You may not want to use these distractions because they're too painful, but my response would be that they're not as painful as the emotions you're allowing to fill your mind. If what you've been doing hasn't been working, try this a few times. It's like having someone follow you around with an electric cattle prod and giving you a shock every time you think a negative thought.

WD Session

If those distractions don't work, try attacking your worries, fears, and depression directly. Schedule a worry and depression time for yourself. We will call it a WD session. Let's say you have reserved the noon hour for your WD session. When you get up in the morning and think about your worries, anxiety, or depression, write down your thoughts on a piece of paper and say to yourself, *I can't deal with these till noon.* Then get on with other tasks.

If you encounter any worry, anxiety, or depression after 1:00 p.m., do the same thing. Write down the thoughts on a piece of paper and tell yourself, *I can't deal with these issues until noon tomorrow.* Then keep that commitment to yourself. Even if you wake up in the night, jot down a few notes and put off thinking about them till your next WD session.

By doing this, your worries, anxiety, and depression begin to lose their grasp on your emotions. You begin controlling your feelings rather than allowing your feelings to control you. By setting your WD session for the noon hour, it will most likely fall during your lunch time. Your body will become hungry, which helps to shorten the WD time. Or a friend may want to go to lunch with you. You might wonder when you'll get a time to deal with your worries and depression. Hello! You have been dealing with them for a long time. Has it been working?

PI Session

If you would like to wage another war on worry, anxiety, and depression, you can use what is called a Paradoxical Intention session. This is similar to a WD session but varies in this sense: During the PI session, you deliberately try to get depressed. You tell yourself, *Okay, it's time for me to be worried, anxious, and depressed. I'm going to go for the gusto and see how deep I can drop my feelings.* You can guess what happens. It doesn't work.

Mood Inventory

Creating an inventory of your moods might be another good way to deal with your emotions. Try writing down your answers to these questions in a journal:

1. I worry and am anxious and depressed about...

2. The top three things I'm concerned about are...

3. The situations that trigger my worry, anxiety, and depression are...

4. The worst possible things that could happen as a result of my top three concerns are...

5. What will most likely happen with my top three concerns?

6. What would be the best things that could happen as a result of my top three concerns?

7. I think about my top three concerns...

     ❏ seldom   ❏ frequently   ❏ all the time

8. Has my worry, anxiety, or depression helped to resolve or change the outcome of my situations?

     ❏ yes   ❏ no   ❏ uncertain

9. How valid are my perceptions of my problems?

10. What do I get out of all of my worry, anxiety, and depression?

11. Will my worry, anxiety, and depression control the future of my problems?

     ❏ yes   ❏ no   ❏ uncertain

12. What types of things would be better to think about?

13. Am I willing to try to change my thinking and perception about my worries, anxiety, and depression?

     ❏ yes   ❏ no   ❏ uncertain

14. What advice would I give to someone in a similar situation?

15. Ten years from today, how will I look back on what I am facing?

Whack!

You might try getting a "whack in the side of the head." Others have called this an "aha moment." Try looking at your problems through a new set of eyes. Attempt to come up with some alternative interpretations and solutions for the problems you are facing. You can do this by yourself or ask a friend to help you take a different look at what is going on in your life.

To help your "whack in the side of the head" experience, I suggest two movies for you to view. *Elephant Man* is the true story of John Merrick and his attitude toward insurmountable circumstances involving worry, anxiety, and depression. And *The Mission* is a wonderful story of how an individual dealt with anger, guilt, depression, and forgiveness.

Friends

Loneliness creates a great deal of anxiety and depression for many people. The increase of Internet dating services is a testimony of the enormous need to have connection and relationship with another person. Loneliness is different from solitude. Solitude is the joy of being alone; loneliness is the pain of being alone. Some people have a difficult time in this area because they have not created positive friendships. Listed below are a few things to consider in the process of establishing lasting relationships.

> Go oft to the house of your friend, for weeds soon choke an unused path.
>
> SHAKESPEARE

1. Do you look forward to being with the person?

2. How do you feel prior to seeing her?

3. Is she critical or supportive?

4. Is she positive or negative?

5. Does she make hostile or sarcastic remarks?

6. Does she put you down?

7. How do you treat her?

8. How do you feel when you are away from her?

9. Do you feel open in sharing with her?

10. Do you trust her?

11. Do you respect her?

12. Would you seek her out for advice?

13. Are you relieved when she is no longer around?

14. Does she drain you or energize you?

15. Do you put her down?

16. Do you criticize her?

17. Do you feel like a parent around her?

18. Do you take responsibility for her?

19. Do you take her for granted?

20. Does she take you for granted?

21. Do you assume the best for her?

22. Does she assume the best for you?

23. Do you try to keep the relationship fresh?

24. Does she try to keep the relationship fresh?

25. Do you communicate clearly?

26. Do you communicate often?

27. Do you touch freely?

Grief and Resilience

Overcoming anxiety and depression that come from grief and loss takes resiliency—the capacity to cope or adapt in spite of an unfortunate life experience. It is the capability to bounce back and make productive and realistic choices.

Elizabeth Kubler-Ross identified what is called the grief process. It is the emotional roller coaster that takes us from the event of the loss to the acceptance of the loss. It involves five basic stages.

1. Denial—*It can't be true.*

2. Anger—*Why me? This is not right or fair.*

3. Bargaining—*There must be a way out. I'll pray for a miracle.*

4. Depression—*I don't care anymore.*

5. Acceptance—*I'm ready for what may come.*

Are you going through one of the above stages? Take heart; you will live through it. You will learn some lessons and eventually conquer your emotions. And peace will come. The goal of mental health is not necessarily happiness; it is peace and the ability to live in a noble way as an example to others.

Challenging events come into everyone's life. The struggle is to keep a resilient balance of just enough positive support from family, peers, school, church, your community, and your culture, and just enough solitude and independence. Although support may be positive, too much may make you dependent on others for your well-being. You need to be able to stand on your own two feet. On the other hand, too little support can make an individual give up or become angry and withdraw from everyone. Sometimes the individual becomes rebellious and begins to take his emotions out on people through abuse or crime. He becomes angry at society in general. Without some form of resilient balance we tend toward selfishness on two extremes.

Look Better, Feel Better

Get out of the sloppy mode of thinking and dressing. The clothes you wear affect your mood. Your mood will be upbeat, or it will add to your depression. Looking better includes improving your personal hygiene: brushing your teeth, combing your hair, taking a bath, washing your clothes, and getting a sparkle back in your eyes.

Sit and stand up straight. Start looking at people when they talk to you. Learning how to carry yourself in the midst of turmoil and crisis is an important part of mental and emotional health. How are you doing in this area?

Goals

Remember the three important questions: What is going on in your life? How do you feel about it? Do you want to change? Part of the change process involves setting goals.

1. Where would you like to be in your thinking, emotions, and behavior in the next three months?

2. Where would you like to be in the next year?

3. Where would you like to be in the next five years?

Overview of Resiliency

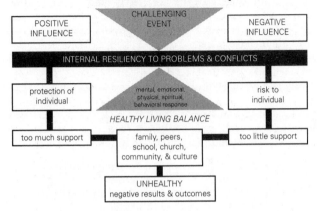

To reach your goals, do you need to say no? Do you need to simplify your life and do away with some of your stress, pressure, and complexity? I have a friend who left a very high-paying job in Los Angeles that was full of stress. The pressures he faced were also putting a great deal of stress on his family. He and his wife talked about what was happening, and they made a decision to move to the country. He took a lower-paying job with decreased responsibilities. The end result was a happier man and a happier family. His decision came about because he had personal and family goals that helped to give him direction.

Goals need to be specific, measurable, realistic, and not overly complex. Keep in mind that the completion of our goals often takes more time than we planned on. It may cost more money and take more energy than we expected. This is the realistic side of goal setting. This is not meant to discourage you, but to prepare you in case you encounter some setbacks along the way.

Start Now

Procrastination breeds anxiety and depression. Often the individual who puts off tasks begins to worry. Guilt from not doing what he should do (or needs to do or would like to do) increases anxiety and can lead to depression.

Charles Michael Schwab was the president of the United States Steel Corporation and then the Bethlehem Steel Corporation. He was a very wealthy and busy man. One day he went to lunch with a friend named Lee Ivy. During the meal, Mr. Schwab shared how busy he was. He was under a great deal of stress and trying to juggle his family life. He casually mentioned that he would give a lot of money to someone who could tell him how to get more things done in a day.

Mr. Ivy took out his pen, wrote a few sentences on a napkin, and gave it to Mr. Schwab. He shared a few thoughts about the note, and then the lunch ended. A month later, Mr. Ivy received a letter from Mr. Schwab. Inside he discovered a check for $25,000. It was in appreciation for the sentence he wrote for Mr. Schwab. Here is what Mr. Ivy wrote:

> Write down the most important things you have to do tomorrow. Now, number them in the order of their true importance. The first thing tomorrow morning, start working on item number one, and stay with it until completed. Then take item number two the same way. Then number three, and so on. Don't worry if you don't complete everything on the schedule. At least you will have completed the most important projects before getting to the less important ones.

Breaking complex tasks into smaller tasks is a beginning. And if you tackle the hardest task first and complete it, everything gets easier from there. If you start with the smallest task first, anxiety and depression can rise as you begin to attack larger and larger tasks.

If your goals require you to make major decisions, sleep on the decisions if possible. Quick decisions can bring about negative results if we are not careful. Of course, putting off decisions can also create negative results. Maintain a balance.

You've probably heard people say, "I'm not going to make a decision until I get all of the facts." That sounds good, but if you wait until you get all of the facts, you are no longer making a decision. You're drawing a conclusion. Decisions are made without all the facts. That's why they are called decisions. Anxiety rises in some individuals because they don't want to make the wrong decision. Their hesitation begins to paralyze them with fear, and they make no decision. The whole process frustrates and depresses them.

Fear of failure or fear of rejection often creates anxiety. In this case, we need to chill out and remember that no one is perfect. We all make mistakes. That's why pencils have erasers. We need to learn to make decisions and undertake the things we are responsible for. Completion of these tasks eliminates anxiety, destroys depression, gives us self-confidence, and establishes a sense of peace from finishing something we started.

Have courage for the great sorrows of life and patience for the small ones; and when you have laboriously accomplished your daily task, go to sleep in peace. God is awake.

VICTOR HUGO

Pain

One of the secrets of overcoming anxiety and depression is to learn to make peace with pain. We don't have to look far to see vast amounts of heartache and despair. Newspapers and television programs are filled with stories of fire, flood, earthquakes, and tornados. Natural disasters have disrupted many families worldwide. Theft, murder, rape, child abuse, and other crimes have ripped up the lives of millions. Drugs and alcohol continue to destroy individuals and their loved ones. Cancer, heart disease, and other illnesses strike new people every day. Coworkers are laid off, friends face the devastation of an accident, or loved ones suffer a divorce. Every one of us has experienced the pain of broken or damaged relationships.

If we cannot escape the suffering that humanity experiences, what are we to do? We must learn to face the pain. Evading it or running away from it will not solve anything. We need to confront difficult situations and learn how to grow through legitimate suffering.

To better understand this concept, note the difference between imposed suffering and elected suffering. Imposed suffering comes from life events over which we have no control. A natural disaster is a classic example. We have no control over earthquakes and the damage they produce. We have no control over who will become a type 1 or type 2 diabetic. We have no control over those who would fire us or lay us off of work. All of these experiences are imposed or forced upon us from the outside. We cannot change them. We can only painfully accept them and move on.

Elected suffering also creates agony, but it comes from a different source. It is not imposed on us; it comes from inside us. We create it out of our own thinking process or our own actions. No one forces us to become practicing alcoholics; we choose to drink. No one forces drugs upon us; we choose to take drugs. No one forces us to overeat; we choose to put food in our mouths. No one forces us to divorce our spouses; we choose to divorce them. We choose to look at pornography. We choose to lie. We choose to steal. We choose to cheat. We choose to gossip. We choose to be negative and critical. We choose to be bitter and angry. We choose to hurt others. The responsibility for the pain and misery that comes from elected suffering is ours and ours alone.

> Once we truly know that life is difficult—once we truly understand and accept it—then life is no longer difficult. Because once it is accepted, the fact that life is difficult no longer matters.
>
> M. SCOTT PECK

Another way to look at our choices is to distinguish between *facts* of life and *problems* in life. Facts are the things we cannot change. For example, I cannot change the fact that my wife had cancer. I cannot change the fact that my oldest daughter had to undergo a colostomy because of a doctor's mistake. I cannot change the fact that I have had to bury both of my parents. I cannot change the fact of constant pain because of a head-on collision. None of the above are problems for me. They are simply facts of life. To be fearful, anxious, angry, or depressed about them won't change a thing. To do so would be fruitless.

Problems are different from facts. We can work on our problems. We can overcome or change them. Overeating is a problem. Anger is a problem. Fear is a problem. Worry is a problem. Anxiety is a problem. Depression is a problem. Having a critical spirit is a problem. Problems give us the opportunity to make changes in our thinking and our behavior. When we take responsibility for our problems, we can change and grow. When we shoulder our responsibility, we create hope. Hope generates energy and gives motivation to solve problems.

What is your outlook toward problems? Are you willing to face them? Are you willing to learn from them and grow in maturity? The Bible gives much encouragement for those who want to learn how to deal with problems and difficulties.

We can rejoice, too, when we run into problems and trials, for we know that they are good for us—they help us learn to be patient. And patience develops strength of character in us and helps us trust God more each time we use it until finally our hope and faith are strong and steady. Then, when that happens, we are able to hold our heads high no matter what happens and know that all is well, for we know how dearly God loves us, and we feel this warm love everywhere within us because God has given us the Holy Spirit to fill our hearts with his love (Romans 5:3-5).

What a wonderful God we have—he is the Father of our Lord Jesus Christ, the source of every mercy, and the one who so wonderfully comforts and strengthens us in our hardships and trials. And why does he do this? So that when others are troubled, needing our sympathy and encouragement, we can pass on to them this same help and comfort God has given us. You can be sure that the more we undergo sufferings for Christ, the more he will shower us with his comfort and encouragement (2 Corinthians 1:3-5).

> They sailed. They sailed. Then spoke the mate:
>
> "This mad sea shows its teeth tonight.
>
> He curls his lip, he lies in wait,
>
> With lifted teeth, as if to bite!
>
> Brave admiral, say but one good word;
>
> What shall we do when hope is gone?"
>
> The words leapt like a leaping sword:
>
> "Sail on! sail on! sail on! and on!"
>
> JOAQUIN MILLER

Dear brothers, is your life full of difficulties and temptations? Then be happy, for when the way is rough, your patience has a chance to grow. So let it grow, and don't try to squirm out of your problems. For when your patience is finally in full bloom, then you will be ready for anything, strong in character, full and complete (James 1:2-4).

So be truly glad! There is wonderful joy ahead, even though the going is rough for a while down here. These trials are only

> to test your faith, to see whether or not it is strong and pure. It is being tested as fire tests gold and purifies it—and your faith is far more precious to God than mere gold; so if your faith remains strong after being tried in the test tube of fiery trials, it will bring you much praise and glory and honor on the day of his return (1 Peter 1:6-7).

Have you made peace with pain? Have you come to the place where you have accepted the facts of life that cannot be changed? Or are you still fighting and holding on, thinking they will change? Is it time for you to let go? Is it time for you to take the bridle and bit of reality?

Remember the difference between facts of life and problems. You can work on problems. Maybe some issues in your life need a little work, such as your temper or lack of self-control. Perhaps you feel sorry for yourself, procrastinate, or are disorganized. You might be wrapped in worries that you need to strip off. Maybe you struggle with a low self-image or strong perfectionist tendencies.

Each week has 168 hours. We devote about 56 of them to sleeping and about 21 hours for eating and preparing food. If we work a 40-hour week and spend about 3 hours a week commuting, that leaves us about 48 hours for accomplishing other tasks. Why not spend a few hours working on issues that bring about anxiety and depression? Whatever difficulties you are facing, today is the day to get started on effecting change.

- Let go of blame.
- Let go of failure.
- Let go of the past.
- Push through pain.
- Live in the present.
- Let go of the future.
- Relax for a change.
- Let go of the habit of hurrying.
- Get a physical checkup.
- Let go of demands on yourself.
- Take time for beauty and nature.
- Become involved with physical labor.

- Take the god of medicine off of the pedestal of mental health.
- Join something—a college class, hobby club, church, volunteer organization, art class, photography club, or gardening group.

It is not the critic who counts; not the man who points out how the strong man stumbles, or where the doer of deeds could have done them better. The credit belongs to the man who is actually in the arena, whose face is marred by dust and sweat and blood; who strives valiantly; who errs, and comes short again and again, because there is no effort without error and shortcoming; but who does actually strive to do the deeds; who knows the great enthusiasms, the great devotions; who spends himself in a worthy cause; who at the best knows in the end the triumph of high achievement, and who at the worst, if he fails, at least fails while daring greatly, so that his place shall never be with those cold and timid souls who know neither victory nor defeat.

THEODORE ROOSEVELT

14

The REFORMED MIND

Thinking and Acting According to the Bible

❖

He who reforms himself,
has done much toward reforming others;
and one reason why the world is not reformed, is, because
each would have others make a beginning, and never thinks
of himself doing it.

THOMAS ADAMS

TIMID AS A MOUSE were my first thoughts as Shannon entered the office and sat down in the swivel rocking chair. Almost immediately the chair began to move back and forth. She was nervous, and the rocking seemed to help her release some of her tension. She held her hands tightly together in her lap. I also noticed she was shaking slightly. I knew I needed to help her relax and be a little more at ease.

"Good morning, Shannon. I'm glad you dropped by to see me. It's been a little cool today. If you would like, you can use that afghan in the basket next to the chair." She glanced at the basket and hesitated for a moment. She then reached down, drew it out, and covered herself.

Before long, she began enjoying the warmth of the afghan. Her rocking began to decrease, and I could sense she was feeling more secure.

Shannon began to share with me the anxiety she was feeling. "I don't know what to do. I'm scared of almost everything. I don't like to go outside of my apartment. I only do it because I have to go to work or to buy some food. I don't like to be in crowds—they make me feel claustrophobic. I feel my heart pounding like it's going to burst out of my chest. All of my muscles seem to get tense. I especially feel it in my stomach. It feels like it's tied up in knots, and the butterflies are having a convention. My mouth dries up. And then I begin to perspire, and I think everyone will notice. The only place I feel safe is at home with the doors locked and the lights turned on. I even leave some lights on when I go to sleep. I'm afraid someone will break in."

"Will keeping the lights on help to keep someone from breaking in?" I asked, trying to slow her rapid speech down a little.

"I don't know. Well, I hope so. I suppose if someone wanted to get in, he could, but the lights being on might scare him away. At least the light helps me feel better." Her speech started to pick up speed again.

Like many people, Shannon was filled with fear. She worried about the future. She worried about her health. She worried about her job. She worried about what people thought of her. She worried that no one would want to marry her and that she would be single the rest of her life. She worried that she might be going crazy. She worried that God was upset with her. There were very few things that she didn't worry about.

"Shannon, you mentioned that you thought God might be upset with you. Do you believe in God?"

Her rocking stopped for a moment. "Oh, sure I do. I've always believed in God, even when I was a little girl."

"What do you think about the Bible?"

Shannon's head began to move up and down. "I think it's God's Word. I learned that in Sunday school."

"Are you aware of the verse in 1 Peter 5:7 that says, 'Cast all your anxiety on him because he cares for you?'"

"I think I've heard that before."

"Have you been casting all of your anxiety on God?"

Shannon began to shake her head back and forth. "No. I guess I really hadn't thought about it."

"Do you like to fly in an airplane?"

Shannon looked at me with a puzzled look. "No! I can't stand planes. I'm afraid they're going to crash."

"Let's pretend you were going to fly on a plane, and this event takes place before 9/11. You're nervous about getting on the plane. You don't like the narrow aisle. You feel claustrophobic about how close together the seats are. You don't like the seat belt around you because you might want to escape.

"You finally find your seat, and it's next to a window, overlooking one of the wings. The engines begin to whine, and the plane is backed up by a little red truck. The airplane then begins to taxi onto the runway. Suddenly, you can't take it any longer. You unbuckle your seat belt and step across the people next to you and into the aisle. You run down the aisle to the door of the cockpit, pound on it as hard as you can, and yell for the captain to open the door. The engines begin to die down, and the plane pulls to a stop. The captain opens the door to see what the commotion is all about. He looks at you with a surprised and concerned look on his face.

"Then you say, 'I was sitting in the back next to the wing, and I wanted to remind you to use the flaps to help us get off of the ground. You know we can't take off without the flaps.'

"Shannon, what do you think the captain would think about what you did?"

"He'd think I was crazy and kick me off the plane."

"Why would he think that?"

"Because he's a pilot and has flown hundreds of times. He doesn't need me to tell him how to do it."

Shannon and I talked for a little while, and soon she realized she was doing the same thing with God. He is the captain, and He knows what He's doing. He doesn't need us to tell Him how to fly our lives. We don't accomplish anything by worrying about the daily issues in our lives. God knows when to put up the flaps and raise us to a new understanding.

> Therefore I tell you, do not worry about your life, what you will eat or drink; or about your body, what you will wear. Is not life more important than food, and the body more important than clothes? Look at the birds of the air; they do not sow or reap or store away in barns, and yet your heavenly Father feeds them. Are you not much more valuable than they? Who of you by worrying can add a single hour to his life?

> And why do you worry about clothes? See how the lilies of the field grow. They do not labor or spin. Yet I tell you that not even Solomon in all his splendor was dressed like one of these. If that is how God clothes the grass of the field, which is here today and tomorrow is thrown into the fire, will he not much more clothe you, O you of little faith? So do not worry, saying,

> "What shall we eat?" or "What shall we drink?" or "What shall we wear?" For the pagans run after all these things, and your heavenly Father knows that you need them. But seek first his kingdom and his righteousness, and all these things will be given to you as well. Therefore do not worry about tomorrow, for tomorrow will worry about itself. Each day has enough trouble of its own (Matthew 6:25-34 NIV).

We often become like the disciples who were in the boat with Jesus when a furious squall came up. The waves broke over the boat and threatened to swamp it. Jesus was asleep on a pillow in the stern of the boat. The disciples rushed to Him and woke Him up. They said, "Teacher, don't you care if we drown?"

Can you imagine that? They were waking up the Creator of the universe, thinking that He didn't know what was happening.

Jesus got up and rebuked the wind and the waves, and the storm ceased. He then said to his disciples, "Why are you so afraid? Do you still have no faith?"

The disciples were scared to death by what happened. They said to each other, "Who is this? Even the wind and the waves obey him!" (Mark 4:36-41 NIV).

You may feel as if you're on the rough sea of life. You may think the waves of anxiety and depression are going to sink you, and you'll drown in despair. But the good news is that the Creator of the universe is not asleep. He sees the waves of adversity you're facing. He knows you're terrified about your future. He wants to say, "Peace, be still," and to quiet the tempest in your life.

> Said the robin to the sparrow,
> "I should really like to know
> Why these anxious human beings
> Rush about and worry so."
> Said the sparrow to the robin:
> "Friend, I think that it must be,
> That they have no heavenly Father
> Such as cares for you and me."
>
> Elizabeth Cheney

"I'm glad you could see me, Doc. I don't know what to do. I just got out of jail last week, and my marriage is a mess." Darren had barely shaken my hand when he started talking. I motioned for him to sit on the couch.

"Darren, help me understand what's going on in your life. Why were you in jail?"

"I hit my wife, and she called the cops. It was the second time. I had been drinking, and we got in an argument."

"What led up to your argument?"

"I was laid off from work two months ago, and I've been depressed and didn't feel like working. The bills keep coming, and we're running out of money. Kay keeps nagging me about finding some work. I was just tired of hearing about it, and I guess I lost my temper."

Many men who become depressed have a tendency to be stoic and stuff their emotions deep inside. They have a difficult time putting into words how they are feeling. Often they will act out their emotions through anger and domestic violence. Adding alcohol to the mix can make it quite explosive. Men don't want to be seen as weak and helpless. They may resort to overcontrolling situations where they feel they are losing control.

Darren was under a great deal of stress because he lost his job. It had affected his self-image and his financial standing. The unfairness of the loss angered him, and he took it out on his family and almost anyone who got in his way. His depression increased when he hit his wife. He was now angry with himself and with the police. He was an emotional time bomb. He was caught in a downward spiral of depression, disruptive behavior, despair, and discouragement.

The psalmist has a very graphic way of describing his depression.

> Hear my prayer, O LORD;
>   let my cry for help come to you.
> Do not hide your face from me
>   when I am in distress.
> Turn your ear to me;
>   when I call, answer me quickly.
> For my days vanish like smoke;
>   my bones burn like glowing embers.
> My heart is blighted and withered like grass;
>   I forget to eat my food.
> Because of my loud groaning

I am reduced to skin and bones.
I am like a desert owl,
    like an owl among the ruins.
I lie awake; I have become
    like a bird alone on a roof.
All day long my enemies taunt me;
    those who rail against me use my name as a curse.
For I eat ashes as my food
    and mingle my drink with tears
because of your great wrath,
    for you have taken me up and thrown me aside.
My days are like the evening shadow;
    I wither away like grass (Psalm 102:1-11 NIV).

The Bible is filled with men who struggled with depression: Cain, Moses, Elijah, David, Jonah, Judas, and others. David became depressed on several occasions. In Psalm 55 David recounts how his feelings of depression were affecting him.

My heart is in anguish within me;
    the terrors of death assail me.
Fear and trembling have beset me;
    horror has overwhelmed me.
I said, "Oh, that I had the wings of a dove!
    I would fly away and be at rest—
I would flee far away
    and stay in the desert (Psalm 55:4-7 NIV).

On another occasion David was depressed because of *guilt* in his life. He had committed adultery with Bathsheba and had ordered that her husband, Uriah, be killed in battle. His depression and guilt came to a head when Nathan the prophet confronted him with his sin. In despair he cried out to God in Psalm 51:1-12 (NIV):

Have mercy on me, O God,
    according to your unfailing love;
according to your great compassion
    blot out my transgressions.
Wash away all my iniquity
    and cleanse me from my sin.

For I know my transgressions,
    and my sin is always before me.
Against you, you only, have I sinned
    and done what is evil in your sight...
Cleanse me with hyssop, and I will be clean;
    wash me, and I will be whiter than snow.
Let me hear joy and gladness;
    let the bones you have crushed rejoice.
Hide your face from my sins
    and blot out all my iniquity.
Create in me a pure heart, O God,
    and renew a steadfast spirit within me.
Do not cast me from your presence
    or take your Holy Spirit from me.
Restore to me the joy of your salvation
    and grant me a willing spirit, to sustain me.

If you are encountering depression, is it from guilt? Have you done something that you know in your heart was wrong? Or have you not done something you should have? In those cases our conscience will not let us rest until we deal with the matter. Guilt will morph itself into anxiety and depression, and depression will eat away like a cancer. David describes this process as his bones being crushed.

Joy and gladness will only come back when we seek forgiveness from God and the people we may have injured. Only then can God cleanse our heart and can we experience freedom. But sad to say, many will not admit they have done anything wrong. Their pride will not allow themselves to admit failure, wrongdoing, or sin.

Sin

Now, there's an interesting word—*sin*. According to Webster, sin is "any voluntary transgression of a religious law or moral principle." But according to the Bible, it includes actions that are willfully committed and those that occur from neglect.

In 1973, Karl Menninger wrote a controversial book entitled *Whatever Became of Sin?* In that volume he discussed society's attempt to call misbehavior a sickness. I think we could still ask that same question today. Whatever became of sin?

In our present society, certain words are not politically correct. Many people would like to see them removed from the dictionary because they're too black and white, too judgmental, too disparaging or critical. They are too intolerant. Here are a few of the words that many people avoid when describing other people's behavior:

bad	deviant	fiendish	ungodly
degenerate	diabolical	immoral	vicious
depraved	evil	sinful	wicked

Instead of calling behavior evil or sinful, many people use other, more tolerant words that can soften the harsh, judgmental, and intolerant tone of the word *sin.*

blunder	goof	mistake	screwup
boo-boo	indiscretion	moral turpitude	slipup
error	lapse	naughty	transgression
fault	misconduct	omission	weakness
foul-up	misstep	out of line	wrongdoing

Regardless of our attempt to soften the word *sin,* every day the newspapers, magazines, television, and Internet provide examples of it. Some wicked and evil people would have you believe they are just sick, misled, or just simply misunderstood.

Guilt

Another word that is being shunned today is *guilt.* People don't like to be accused of being guilty. "How can you call me guilty? You're not perfect either. You're just being judgmental. Everyone makes mistakes, even you."

To admit guilt for something we've done requires taking responsibility and ownership for our words and actions. Erica Jong comments on this when she says, "Take your life in your own hands, and what happens? A terrible thing: no one to blame." Bob Goddard said, "To err is human. To blame it on the other guy is even more human." Others have mentioned that fear is the tax that conscience pays to guilt.

Of course, some people go around feeling guilty for everything that happens whether they were involved or not. This behavior gets attention (which they are seeking) as others come to their rescue, telling them that it wasn't their fault, and they get their 15 minutes of fame. Josh Billings said, "The quickest way to take the starch out of a fellow who is always blaming himself is to agree with him."

When you blame others, you give up your power to change. Arnold Lazarus addressed this topic when he said, "As long as we incorrectly blame outside sources for our miseries, it remains impossible to do much about them. However, if we realize that we upset ourselves over the things that happen to us, we can work at changing."

The concept of blaming others and not taking responsibility was inherited from Adam. When God confronted him for his disobedience, Adam said, "The woman you put here with me—she gave me some fruit from the tree, and I ate it." (It was her fault.) Eve was not to be outdone by her husband. When God questioned her about the same issue she responded, "The serpent deceived me, and I ate." (It was the serpent's fault.)

God placed a unique item into the heart of every man and woman— the conscience. It's that still small inner voice that either accuses us or excuses us for our thoughts, words, and behavior. Someone has said that conscience is the inner voice that tells you the IRS might check your tax return.

When the conscience accuses us, we feel guilty. Long ago, Seneca spoke of the effects of guilt. "Let wickedness escape as it may at the bar [a court of judgment]; it never fails of doing justice upon itself, for every guilty person is his own hangman."

When people do not admit their guilt, all kinds of fears and anxieties arise. Close behind the load of anxiety comes an unrelenting depression. William Wordsworth caught this concept in his striking couplet, "From the body of one guilty deed a thousand ghostly fears and haunting thoughts proceed." Mark Twain said it this way: "Conscience takes up more room than all the rest of a person's insides."

One might then ask, how do we deal with the guilty conscience? Ideally, we take seven important steps. Unfortunately, many people do not complete all of the steps.

Responsibility. The first step is to take responsibility. This means to admit and own your thoughts, words, and behaviors. I thought it. I spoke it. I did it. Some people do not even proceed up the first step.

Regret. This comes in the form of sorrow. I realize and admit that what I thought, spoke, and did was wrong. I shouldn't have done that.

Remorse. This is a stronger form of sorrow. It is a deeply felt mourning or bitter regret for thoughts, words, or deeds. The people who have been hurt or injured by your words or actions seem to be able to pick up the spirit of remorse better than regret and sorrow. This is because some people are sorrowful only because they were caught and regret simply that what they said or did was found out. In these cases even though people will say they're sorry, something about their admission does not ring clear.

Repentance. This remorse is so deep that it actually causes people to turn around and change their thoughts, words, and behavior. Repentance is a military word that refers to an about-face. It is a complete reversal of direction. This is an inward change that becomes visible to everyone around. It is not just a momentary turnaround. It is a permanent transformation.

Restitution. This is a difficult and complicated step. Restitution is paying back in full for damages incurred. If I break your bicycle, restitution would mean buying you another one of equal or greater value. That's not too difficult. It's pretty straightforward.

But what if I damaged your reputation? How can I repair that? What if I ran over your child with my car? How could I replace your child? Some circumstances are not as straightforward as replacing a bicycle. In these cases, we can only express a sincere apology, accompanied by honest and believable remorse.

In the case of damaging a reputation or hurting a number of people, restitution may take the form of humbly going to the people involved, admitting your misdeed to them, and asking for forgiveness. Some may grant you forgiveness, and some may suggest that you go to the hot place. That is not the issue. The point is that you go and attempt to resolve the issue regardless of the outcome.

What are you to do if the individual has moved or has passed away? In the Old Testament, when recompense could not be made to a person directly, the recompense was brought to the temple as an offering to God and was left with Him. Maybe that is what you need to do.

Release. When the first five steps have been completed, you will enjoy a release of freedom in your life. You have done everything humanly possible to take responsibility, to express regret, to experience remorse, to repent and change your ways, and to make restitution. Only then will you be free in your spirit. You will be able to live with yourself and others with a clear conscience.

Often when relationships have been damaged, the individuals responsible only go through the first four steps. They do the first four sincerely and actually repent and change their behavior. But they do not experience complete freedom in their spirit because they do not attempt to make restitution. It is a very difficult step, and it is stifled by fear and pride.

> Forgiveness is the fragrance the violet sheds on the heel that has crushed it.
>
> MARK TWAIN

Reconciliation. The first six steps lay the groundwork for reconciliation. They help to make possible the restoration of relationships and friendships. However, I must be honest and say that for several reasons, restoration and reconciliation do not always take place.

The person may have died or moved away. The wounded person may not be willing or able to forgive you. You cannot force forgiveness. It must be given freely. Or perhaps the person forgives you for what you did but no longer wants to have a relationship with you. I can learn to forgive the man who molested my daughter years ago, but he certainly will never be my bosom buddy. Nor should he be.

Greed

King Ahab became sullen and depressed because of his greed. He wanted to own a vineyard belonging to a man named Naboth. Naboth would not sell the vineyard to the king, so Ahab went home and pouted.

> So Ahab went home, sullen and angry because Naboth the Jezreelite had said, "I will not give you the inheritance of my fathers." He lay on his bed sulking and refused to eat.
>
> His wife Jezebel came in and asked him, "Why are you so sullen? Why won't you eat?"
>
> He answered her, "Because I said to Naboth the Jezreelite, 'Sell me your vineyard; or if you prefer, I will give you another vineyard in its place.' But he said, 'I will not give you my vineyard.'"

Jezebel his wife said, "Is this how you act as king over Israel? Get up and eat! Cheer up. I'll get you the vineyard of Naboth the Jezreelite."

So she wrote letters in Ahab's name, placed his seal on them, and sent them to the elders and nobles who lived in Naboth's city with him. In those letters she wrote:

Proclaim a day of fasting and seat Naboth in a prominent place among the people. But seat two scoundrels opposite him and have them testify that he has cursed both God and the king. Then take him out and stone him to death (1 Kings 21:4-10 NIV).

Hatred

The prophet Jonah became depressed because of his hatred. He became so angry that he wanted God to take his life. God had told Jonah to go to the town of Nineveh and preach a message of repentance. Jonah hated the Assyrians and didn't want to do it. Nineveh was originally founded by Nimrod, a great-grandson of Noah, and the Assyrians were very fierce and warlike. Jonah had good reasons for not wanting to go to Ninevah.

Jonah did not want to see these wicked people repent. He wanted to see them punished for all their viciousness. When God did forgive the Ninevites,

Jonah was greatly displeased and became angry. He prayed to the LORD, "O LORD, is this not what I said when I was still at home? That is why I was so quick to flee to Tarshish. I knew that you are a gracious and compassionate God, slow to anger and abounding in love, a God who relents from sending calamity. Now, O LORD, take away my life, for it is better for me to die than to live" (Jonah 4:1-3 NIV).

Hatred and revenge were in Jonah's heart, and they grew into a deep depression. Might you be experiencing anxiety and depression because of some hatred, resentment, or desire to inflict revenge on someone? Taking pills will not take away those destructive emotions. Let go of your anger, hatred, and desire for retaliation.

Pride and Envy

Haman was filled with pride and envy. Even though he was a man of wealth and prestige, he became depressed. He was angry because a Jew named Mordecai would not bow down to him.

> Calling together his friends and Zeresh, his wife, Haman boasted to them about his vast wealth, his many sons, and all the ways the king had honored him and how he had elevated him above the other nobles and officials. "And that's not all," Haman added. "I'm the only person Queen Esther invited to accompany the king to the banquet she gave. And she has invited me along with the king tomorrow. But all this gives me no satisfaction as long as I see that Jew Mordecai sitting at the king's gate" (Esther 5:10-13 NIV).

Stress

Moses became depressed because there was too much stress in his life. He was overloaded and angry with God.

> Moses heard the people of every family wailing, each at the entrance to his tent. The LORD became exceedingly angry, and Moses was troubled. He asked the LORD, "Why have you brought this trouble on your servant? What have I done to displease you that you put the burden of all these people on me? Did I conceive all these people? Did I give them birth? Why do you tell me to carry them in my arms, as a nurse carries an infant, to the land you promised on oath to their forefathers? Where can I get meat for all these people? They keep wailing to me, 'Give us meat to eat!' I cannot carry all these people by myself; the burden is too heavy for me. If this is how you are going to treat me, put me to death right now—If I have found favor in your eyes—and do not let me face my own ruin" (Numbers 11:10-15 NIV).

Have you ever been angry with God? Have you ever wondered why you are facing your particular trials? Do you feel stressed-out and overloaded by the burdens you are carrying? Do you feel as if God is punishing you? You're not the first one to feel that way. Try to imagine being the leader of two million people who were angry with you.

Come to me, all you who are weary and burdened, and I will give you rest. Take my yoke upon you and learn from me, for I am gentle and humble in heart, and you will find rest for your souls. For my yoke is easy and my burden is light" (Matthew 11:28-30 NIV).

Lust

Amnon was the son of King David. He fell in love with his beautiful half-sister. He became anxious, frustrated, and depressed because of lust.

Amnon became frustrated to the point of illness on account of his sister Tamar, for she was a virgin, and it seemed impossible for him to do anything to her.

Now Amnon had a friend named Jonadab son of Shimeah, David's brother. Jonadab was a very shrewd man. He asked Amnon, "Why do you, the king's son, look so haggard morning after morning? Won't you tell me?"

Amnon said to him, "I'm in love with Tamar, my brother Absalom's sister." "Go to bed and pretend to be ill," Jonadab said. "When your father comes to see you, say to him, 'I would like my sister Tamar to come and give me something to eat. Let her prepare the food in my sight so I may watch her and then eat it from her hand.'"

So Amnon lay down and pretended to be ill. When the king came to see him, Amnon said to him, "I would like my sister Tamar to come and make some special bread in my sight, so I may eat from her hand."

David sent word to Tamar at the palace: "Go to the house of your brother Amnon and prepare some food for him." So Tamar went to the house of her brother Amnon, who was lying down. She took some dough, kneaded it, made the bread in his sight and baked it. Then she took the pan and served him the bread, but he refused to eat.

"Send everyone out of here," Amnon said. So everyone left him. Then Amnon said to Tamar, "Bring the food here into my bedroom so I may eat from your hand." And Tamar took the bread she had prepared and brought it to her brother Amnon in his bedroom. But when she took it to him to eat, he grabbed her and said, "Come to bed with me, my sister."

"Don't, my brother!" she said to him. "Don't force me. Such a thing should not be done in Israel! Don't do this wicked thing. What about me? Where could I get rid of my disgrace? And what about you? You would be like one of the wicked fools in Israel. Please speak to the king; he will not keep me from being married to you." But he refused to listen to her, and since he was stronger than she, he raped her.

Then Amnon hated her with intense hatred. In fact, he hated her more than he had loved her. Amnon said to her, "Get up and get out!"

"No!" she said to him. "Sending me away would be a greater wrong than what you have already done to me."

But he refused to listen to her. He called his personal servant and said, "Get this woman out of here and bolt the door after her." So his servant put her out and bolted the door after her. She was wearing a richly ornamented robe, for this was the kind of garment the virgin daughters of the king wore. Tamar put ashes on her head and tore the ornamented robe she was wearing. She put her hand on her head and went away, weeping aloud as she went (2 Samuel 13:2-19 NIV).

Consider the frustration, anxiety, anger, and depression that has been brought about by unbridled sexual desire. Think of the lives that have been damaged and destroyed, the guilt and remorse that have been experienced. Many people go from doctor to doctor, seeking advice for their troubled consciences. When relief does not come, they turn to alcohol and drugs. Some struggle with their grief and guilt and choose to withdraw from themselves and society. Their mind quits functioning rationally as an escape from their emotions and pain.

Are a few moments of sexual gratification worth this heartache?

Several years ago, my wife and I invited six couples to a dessert get-together. Late in the evening, the conversation somehow turned to the discussion of sexual abuse of younger people. Every one of the seven women in the room had experienced some form of sexual abuse. A few were abused by family members, and others were molested by people outside of their family.

Pills will not heal this hurt, nor will alcohol. Healing comes about when these issues are laid at the feet of Jesus. That is where one finds freedom, forgiveness, and peace.

> For the eyes of the Lord are intently watching all who live good lives, and he gives attention when they cry to him. But the Lord has made up his mind to wipe out even the memory of evil men from the earth. Yes, the Lord hears the good man when he calls to him for help and saves him out of all his troubles.
>
> The Lord is close to those whose hearts are breaking; he rescues those who are humbly sorry for their sins. The good man does not escape all troubles—he has them too. But the Lord helps him in each and every one. Not one of his bones is broken.
>
> Calamity will surely overtake the wicked; heavy penalties are meted out to those who hate the good. But as for those who serve the Lord, he will redeem them; everyone who takes refuge in him will be freely pardoned (Psalm 34:15-22).

Anger and Jealousy

Cain became angry when God did not accept his offering. He then became jealous when God did receive his brother Abel's offering. The anger and jealousy led to depression, which was apparent in his facial expression. We find the story in Genesis 4:2-16:

> Now Abel kept flocks, and Cain worked the soil. In the course of time Cain brought some of the fruits of the soil as an offering to the Lord. But Abel brought fat portions from some of the firstborn of his flock. The Lord looked with favor on Abel and his offering, but on Cain and his offering he did not look with favor. So Cain was very angry, and his face was downcast. [Notice the classic signs of depression.]
>
> Then the Lord said to Cain, "Why are you angry? Why is your face downcast? If you do what is right, will you not be accepted? But if you do not do what is right, sin is crouching at your door; it desires to have you, but you must master it."

Many of our problems would be eliminated if we would simply do what we know we should be doing. We don't have to experience emotional turmoil if we do the right thing. The other side of the coin is this: If we do the wrong thing, we will experience negative consequences. This is a cause-and-effect relationship. Whatsoever a man sows, he shall also reap.

> Now Cain said to his brother Abel, "Let's go out to the field." And while they were in the field, Cain attacked his brother Abel and killed him.

This is premeditated murder. Sin rarely occurs without some previous preparation. Cain had been thinking about ending his brother's life.

> Then the LORD said to Cain, "Where is your brother Abel?"
>
> "I don't know," he replied. "Am I my brother's keeper?"

One of the first reactions to being caught doing something wrong is to lie, to cover it up, or to distract the accuser. We try to rationalize and justify what we do. Your children probably demonstrate this.

> The LORD said, "What have you done? Listen! Your brother's blood cries out to me from the ground. Now you are under a curse and driven from the ground, which opened its mouth to receive your brother's blood from your hand. When you work the ground, it will no longer yield its crops for you. You will be a restless wanderer on the earth."

People who do not deal with their sins will begin to wander mentally and emotionally just as Cain wandered geographically.

> Cain said to the LORD, "My punishment is more than I can bear. Today you are driving me from the land, and I will be hidden from your presence; I will be a restless wanderer on the earth, and whoever finds me will kill me."

Reread what Cain said. He used the personal pronouns *my, I,* and *me* seven times. At no point did he admit his wrong or seek forgiveness. He was only concerned about how the punishment would affect him. This is a good example of what many people do. They demonstrate sorrow—that they were caught and have to undergo punishment—but they do not demonstrate any remorse or ownership for their actions.

> But the LORD said to him, "Not so; if anyone kills Cain, he will suffer vengeance seven times over." Then the LORD put a mark on Cain so that no one who found him would kill him.

So Cain went out from the LORD's presence and lived in the land of Nod, east of Eden.

Like many people who will not face their wrong actions, Cain began to wander. He went away from the presence of God and did not return. Many people do the same thing. They struggle with unnecessary guilt, anxiety, and depression. They depart from the presence of God—the One who can give them peace and forgiveness.

Jesus, Our Example

We are told in Hebrews that Jesus faced the same issues we face. The only difference is that He did not sin. He was born into poverty. He was raised in obscurity. He grew tired and felt stress. He became bone weary caring for others and had to rest and eat. He cried over Lazarus and wept over Jerusalem. His friends betrayed Him. He underwent physical pain from beatings and death on the cross. He died alone while He bore on His shoulders all the sins of the world. I don't think our problems will come close to what He experienced in this world. The writer of Hebrews suggests that we look to Jesus as our example in this race of life.

> Therefore then, since we are surrounded by so great a cloud of witnesses [who have borne testimony to the Truth], let us strip off and throw aside every encumbrance (unnecessary weight) and that sin which so readily (deftly and cleverly) clings to and entangles us, and let us run with patient endurance and steady and active persistence the appointed course of the race that is set before us, looking away [from all that will distract] to Jesus, Who is the Leader and the Source of our faith [giving the first incentive for our belief] and is also its Finisher, [bring it to maturity and perfection]. He, for the joy [of obtaining the prize] that was set before Him, endured the cross, despising and ignoring the shame, and is now seated at the right hand of the throne of God. Just think of Him Who endured from sinners such grievous opposition and bitter hostility against Himself [reckon up and consider it all in comparison with your trials], so that you may not grow weary or exhausted, losing heart and relaxing and fainting in your minds. You have not yet struggled and fought agonizingly against sin, nor have you yet resisted and withstood to the point of pouring out your [own] blood (Hebrews 12:1-4 AMP).

The writer of Hebrews goes on to suggest that we can come to Jesus with all of our hurts and longings. We do not have to bear our anxiety and depression alone. Jesus will come alongside us, lift us out of the pit of despair, and place our feet on the solid rock of His love.

> Therefore, since we have a great high priest who has gone through the heavens, Jesus the Son of God, let us hold firmly to the faith we profess. For we do not have a high priest who is unable to sympathize with our weaknesses, but we have one who has been tempted in every way, just as we are—yet was without sin. Let us then approach the throne of grace with confidence, so that we may receive mercy and find grace to help us in our time of need (Hebrews 4:14-16 NIV).

You may wonder if Jesus really experienced anxiety and the effects of depression without sinning. The answer is yes, He did. Read it for yourself, and try to imagine being there.

> Then Jesus went with his disciples to a place called Gethsemane, and he said to them, "Sit here while I go over there and pray." He took Peter and the two sons of Zebedee along with him, and he began to be sorrowful and troubled. Then he said to them, "My soul is overwhelmed with sorrow to the point of death. Stay here and keep watch with me."
>
> Going a little farther, he fell with his face to the ground and prayed, "My Father, if it is possible, may this cup be taken from me. Yet not as I will, but as you will."
>
> Then he returned to his disciples and found them sleeping. "Could you men not keep watch with me for one hour?" he asked Peter. "Watch and pray so that you will not fall into temptation. The spirit is willing, but the body is weak."
>
> He went away a second time and prayed, "My Father, if it is not possible for this cup to be taken away unless I drink it, may your will be done" (Matthew 26:36-42 NIV).

I had been meeting with Lamar for several weeks. He had a great deal of anxiety and believed that he had committed the unpardonable sin.

> I tell you the truth, all the sins and blasphemies of men will be forgiven them. But whoever blasphemes against the Holy

Spirit will never be forgiven; he is guilty of an eternal sin (Mark 3:28-29 NIV).

I shared with him that the mere fact that he was concerned about it signified that he hadn't committed it. For if a person did commit that sin, he certainly wouldn't worry about it. I shared with him a quote from Louis Berkhof:

> This sin consists in the conscious, malicious, and willful rejection and slander, against evidence and conviction, of the testimony of the Holy Spirit respecting the grace of God in Christ, attributing it out of hatred and enmity to the Prince of Darkness…In committing that sin man willfully, maliciously, and intentionally attributes what is clearly recognized as the work of God to the influence and operation of Satan.

That discussion did not end his anxiety and depression. He continued to believe he had committed the unpardonable sin. I began to explore other areas of his life that might have been causing his guilt and fears. We began to make some headway until one day he did not show up for his appointment. We were beginning to get too close to the real issues and difficulties in his life, and he wasn't ready to deal with them. Everyone is on a journey, and we aren't all at the same place and on the same road. Sometimes people aren't ready for change until they experience more struggle and difficulty. Like the young man who had his head shoved under water by Telamon, people must have a strong desire to change before they will.

I don't mean to say I am perfect. I haven't learned all I should even yet, but I keep working toward that day when I will finally be all that Christ saved me for and wants me to be.

No, dear brothers, I am still not all I should be, but I am bringing all my energies to bear on this one thing: Forgetting the past and looking forward to what lies ahead, I strain to reach the end of the race and receive the prize for which God is calling us up to heaven because of what Christ Jesus did for us (Philippians 3:12-14).

15

The REDEMPTIVE MIND

Accepting Peace and Joy from God

❖

Repentance is a hearty sorrow for our past misdeeds, and is a sincere resolution and endeavor, to the utmost of our power, to conform all our actions to the law of God. It does not consist in one single act of sorrow, but in doing works meet for repentance; in a sincere obedience to the law of Christ for the remainder of our lives.

JOHN LOCKE

SEVERAL YEARS AGO I ATTENDED a meeting where a speaker provided each person in the audience with a piece of paper and asked us to tear it into six equal pieces. He then asked us to write down on each piece of paper the six most important things in life to us—one item on each piece of paper.

He mentioned that we might consider things like our health, our spouse, our children, our career, our friendships, our pets, and a number of other items. He then asked us to pick up those pieces of paper and hold them in one hand, fanning them out like playing cards so we could see them.

Next, he talked about how tragedy comes into everyone's life. He mentioned that we can lose our job, we can lose our health, and we can lose our loved ones through death. Everything was going fine until he said, "We are going to imagine that tragedy is going to strike your life today. You will have to give up one of the six things in your hand—never to have it again. Pull out one of the pieces of paper and place it on the table in front of you."

Everyone groaned while trying to make this difficult decision. Then the speaker talked a little more about tragedy and told us that it had just struck a second time. We would have to place another one of the six most important things in our life on the table. With more groans and rumblings, we gave up a second item—never to have it again.

This exercise in priorities continued until we had only one piece of paper in our hands. He said, "I want you to look at the piece of paper in your hand. If it names an item of value or a person you love, I want you to be aware that tragedy could strike and take that important thing from you. Then where would you be? If, however, you have written something like God or a relationship with God, that can never be taken from you."

That turned out to be a very sobering evaluation of what was truly important to us. In turn, I might ask you the same question. If you went through the same exercise, what would you identify as the most important thing in your life? Would it be something that could perish? Would it be a relationship with a loved one that could be lost? Or would your paper point to a relationship with God?

Spiritual matters tend to separate people into three general categories. With which category would you identify yourself?

1. *The whatevers.* Some people couldn't care less about spiritual matters. They do not have any background in religious faith and do not feel a need to develop one. Or if they do have some previous knowledge, they have chosen to reject it.

2. *The ahas.* These are those who may or may not have some spiritual background but are interested in the topic. They are seekers who are open to consider this avenue of life and would like further information.

3. *The thinkers.* These are those who are deeply concerned about spiritual matters. Their emotional and mental health is tied closely to their faith and how it affects their daily life. They strive to grow in their faith and knowledge.

Those who are interested in or deeply concerned about spiritual matters identify with the words of Jesus when He says, "For what profit is it to a man if he gains the whole world, and loses his own soul? Or what will a man give in exchange for his soul?" (Matthew 16:26 NKJV).

Jesus is simply saying that there is more to life than material goods. He warns of the danger of not considering the deeper purposes of life.

Have you ever wondered what life is all about? Have you ever questioned why pain and suffering exist...and why people struggle with anxiety and depression? Have you ever wondered if God has a plan for your life?

Life is not always an easy road. Sometimes we encounter the potholes of difficulties, the bypasses of anxiety, the bumps of pain, and the detours of depression. During these uncomfortable times, we can easily become weary of it all. Are you tired and weary of the pressures in your life and the various troubles you face? Join the club. Many people feel the same way.

> A 1999 Duke University study of four thousand adults found that attendance at a house of worship was related to lower rates of anxiety and depression.
>
> DOUGLAS BLOCH

The Bible reveals that God does care about you and the problems you face. God wants to come to your aid and help you through the tough times—the times that cause anxiety and depression.

Jesus said, "Come to Me, all you who labor and are heavy laden, and I will give you rest. Take My yoke upon you and learn from Me, for I am gentle and lowly in heart, and you will find rest for your souls. For My yoke is easy and My burden is light" (Matthew 11:28-30 NKJV).

How do we come to Jesus? How do we find rest for our souls? How can we experience peace (overcoming anxiety and depression) in the midst of turmoil? Jesus said, "Peace I leave with you, My peace I give to you; not as the world gives do I give to you. Let not your heart be troubled, neither let it be afraid" (John 14:27 NKJV).

Experiencing peace *with* God and the peace *of* God starts with understanding who Jesus is. He is God in a human body. He has come to tell us how to have a relationship with Him that will last for eternity.

When I was in Mongolia, a professor of literature who was a parliament member said to me, "I don't understand your God. He has three faces—Father, Son, and Holy Spirit. How can that be?"

I replied, "You are a professor of literature, are you not?"

"Yes, I am."

"Is the name Shakespeare familiar to you?"

"Of course."

"Are you acquainted with the character Macbeth?"

"Yes, I am."

"Could the character Macbeth ever meet the author Shakespeare?"

He thought for a moment and replied, "No, he could not."

"Ahhh, but he could," I said. "All the author would have to do is to write himself into the play and then introduce himself to Macbeth. That's what God (the Father) did when He wrote Himself into the play of life in the form of the Son (Jesus of Nazareth). He became the God-man."

God is a perfect and holy being. We humans are not perfect; we are not holy. We have imperfections. Try as we may, we often fall short of doing the right thing, saying the right thing, or thinking the right thing. Do you know anyone who is perfect?

This imperfection or sin separates us from a holy God. Now God has a problem. He loves us but must also deal with our sinfulness—our imperfections. He sent His Son to die in our place—to pay our penalty—and to buy us back from the slave market of sinfulness and wickedness.

Jesus bore our sins on the cross for us. He died in our place. He was buried for our cruelty. And He rose from the grave to establish a new life and relationship with God for us. All we have to do is to have faith in this event. The apostle Paul states it this way:

> If you confess with your mouth the Lord Jesus and believe in your heart that God has raised Him from the dead, you will be saved. For with the heart one believes unto righteousness, and with the mouth confession is made unto salvation... For "whoever calls on the name of the Lord shall be saved" (Romans 10:9-10,13 NKJV).

Have you ever done that? If not, you can do it right now. Just put down this book and pray a simple prayer of faith asking Jesus to come into your life. Thank Him for dying in your place. Thank Him for providing a new relationship with God. Ask God to bring people into your life who can help you to grow and learn more about Him. Thank Him for saving you.

Do you remember flying a kite? You ran with the kite held high until the wind caught it and it began to soar into the sky. If you had a long string, the kite rose higher and higher. Eventually, the kite was so high that it seemed to disappear, but you knew the kite was still there because of the tug on the string.

In the same way, God gives a tug on the strings of your heart. Something inside of you senses that God is calling you to make a decision for Christ. You may feel as if I am talking to you personally. That feeling is the tug of God. It's certainly not my writing that's stirring your soul. I'm only a messenger bringing you good news.

When you invite Jesus to come into your life, God sends His Holy Spirit to dwell within. He (the Spirit) will be there to teach you about God. He will support you in tough times. He will help you to endure the pain and suffering that has been ravaging you because of anxiety and depression. He will teach you how to overcome these negative feelings.

To follow up on the decision you just made, look up the following verses in the Bible: Revelation 3:20; Colossians 1:13-14, 27; 1 John 5:11-13; John 6:37; Romans 10:9-13; and Hebrews 13:5. Write down some observations you made from these verses.

Read the Bible every day. Here is a very simple daily Bible study plan.

1. Select one of the books within the Bible that you would like to read. The fourth book in the New Testament, the Gospel of John, is a good book to start with.

2. Read one chapter a day until you are finished with that book.

3. As you read each chapter, make some notes. Try to identify the following:

   • the key verse of the chapter (a central thought)

   • God's commands (a command is something to do)

   • God's promises (a promise is something to believe)

   • a short summary of the chapter

   • personal applications to your daily life

Look up 1 Peter 2:2 and Psalm 119:9,11. Talk to God daily in prayer and keep your relationship with Him growing. Also read 1 John 1:9; Psalm 66:18; and Philippians 4:6-7.

Fellowship with other believers. Get involved in a local church that teaches the truth about Jesus. (See Hebrews 10:25.)

Begin to tell others about Jesus. Learn to serve God wherever you can, and help others grow in their faith. Look up Matthew 28:19-20; Mark 5:19; Acts 1:8; Ephesians 4:29; and 1 Corinthians 10:31. Write down what you learned from reading these Bible verses.

The appendix contains Bible study helps that will encourage your spiritual growth. May your soul be refreshed as you study the Word of God.

By Way of Review

As I mentioned in the beginning, no one single book can explain everything you need to know about anxiety and depression. This has been an attempt to help you take a new look at the subject. My prayer is that the material has provoked thought…that will lead to action…that will help you in the process of overcoming anxiety and depression.

Here are a few of the key thoughts that we covered:

1. Anxiety and depression are common.

2. Anxiety is the number one mental health issue. Depression is the common cold of mental health.

3. Anxiety involves fear about the future. Depression involves hurt, loss, and anger over the past.

4. These are the three important questions in mental health: What's going on? How do you feel about it? Do you want to change?

5. Stress plays an important role in anxiety and depression. Overloaded schedules, damaged relationships, and financial difficulties are just a few of the stress-related issues.

6. Our attitude and perception of life events determines whether we will have a positive spirit or a negative spirit.

7. Exercise, diet, and relaxation are essential when dealing with anxiety and depression.

8. Mental illness is not the same as physical illness. People hurt and feel bad emotionally, but their pain is not caused by a virus, bacteria, or a protozoon. It is not a disease in the traditional sense.

9. Chemical imbalance is almost always a result of our emotions and not a cause of them.

10. A medical model of mental health can lead to discouragement and unresolved issues. A counseling model of mental health promotes responsibility and hope.

11. Drugs that deal with anxiety and depression have many major side effects.

12. Suicide is a selfish act that destroys loved ones who are left behind.

13. People only change when they hurt enough. Until that time they will continue to behave in a manner that gives them some kind of reward or satisfaction—whether the behavior is negative or positive.

14. The more worthy our objective, the harder we will work to achieve it.

15. Four great aids to healing anxiety and depression are sleeping, relaxing, letting time pass, and helping other people rather than focusing on our own misery.

16. We can kill the ANTs (Automatic Negative Thoughts) and replace them with wholesome and positive thinking.

17. We can make peace with pain and learn to accept what we cannot change.

18. Violation of our conscience gives rise to guilt, which in turn creates anxiety and depression.

19. We can let go of the past and stop blaming other people and circumstances. Taking responsibility for our lives is the road to mental health.

20. Clearing our conscience involves accepting responsibility, regretting our violations, feeling remorse, repenting of our misdeeds, making restitution, experiencing release, and becoming reconciled to those we have injured.

21. It is important to evaluate our spiritual life and relationship with God. We find peace of heart and mind by receiving Christ.

22. We grow in our spiritual walk through prayer, Bible study, fellowship with believers, and sharing our faith.

An Often-Overlooked Truth

In our struggles with anxiety and depression, the emotional pain and misery can be intense. During these times we can easily forget a very important truth: *God is not caught off guard by what is happening in your life.*

When you are caught up with anxiety and depression, remind yourself of several of God's attributes. (The verses quoted in the remainder of this chapter are from the NIV.)

God Is Omnipresent

This means that God is everywhere all the time. This is a difficult concept for us to grab hold of. The psalmist described God's omnipresence in Psalm 139:7-10:

> Where can I go from your Spirit?
>   Where can I flee from your presence?
> If I go up to the heavens, you are there;
>   if I make my bed in the depths, you are there.
> If I rise on the wings of the dawn,
>   if I settle on the far side of the sea,
> even there your hand will guide me,
>   your right hand will hold me fast.

God Is Omniscient

This means that God knows everything about everything. He knows about your birth, your struggles, your anxieties, and your depression. He has even mapped out a plan for your life.

> Do you know how the clouds hang poised,
>   those wonders of him who is perfect in knowledge?
> (Job 37:16).

> God is greater than our hearts, and he knows everything
> (1 John 3:20).

> For you created my inmost being;
>   you knit me together in my mother's womb.

I praise you because I am fearfully and wonderfully made;
    your works are wonderful, I know that full well.
My frame was not hidden from you
    when I was made in the secret place.
When I was woven together in the depths of the earth,
    your eyes saw my unformed body.
All the days ordained for me
    were written in your book
    before one of them came to be.
How precious to me are your thoughts, O God!
    How vast is the sum of them!
Were I to count them,
    they would outnumber the grains of sand.
When I awake,
    I am still with you (Psalm 139:13-18).

God Is Omnipotent

This means that God is all-powerful. He is King over all of creation. He is the sovereign ruler. Nothing escapes His power to control—not even anxiety and depression.

> Now to him who is able to do immeasurably more than all we ask or imagine, according to his power that is at work within us, to him be glory in the church and in Christ Jesus throughout all generations, for ever and ever! Amen (Ephesians 3:20-21).

> For nothing is impossible with God (Luke 1:37).

> Whom have I in heaven but you?
>   And earth has nothing I desire besides you.
> My flesh and my heart may fail,
>   but God is the strength of my heart
>   and my portion forever (Psalm 73:25-26).

Take a moment and carefully read through this hymn written by Georg Neumark in 1641. Although it is written in Old English, the message of God's sovereignty and our need to trust Him in times of trouble rings loud and clear.

> If thou but suffer God to guide thee,
> And hope in Him through all thy ways,

He'll give thee strength, whate'er betide thee,
And bear thee through the evil days:
Who trusts in God's unchanging love
Builds on the rock that naught can move.

What can these anxious cares avail thee,
These never-ceasing moans and sighs?
What can it help, if thou bewail thee
O'er each dark moment as it flies?
Our cross and trials do but press
The heavier for our bitterness.

Only be still, and wait His leisure
In cheerful hope, with heart content
To take whate'er thy Father's pleasure
And all-deserving love hath sent;
Nor doubt our inmost wants are known
To Him who chose us for His own.

All are alike before the Highest;
'Tis easy to our God, we know,
To raise thee up though low thou liest,
To make the rich man poor and low;
True wonders still by Him are wrought
Who setteth up and brings to naught.

Sing, pray, and keep His ways unswerving,
So do thine own part faithfully,
And trust His Word, though undeserving,
Thou yet shalt find it true for thee;
God never yet forsook in need
The soul that trusted Him indeed.

God Is Good

This means that all that God is and all that He does is good. It is worthy of approval. It is the final standard for goodness.

> You are good, and what you do is good;
>   teach me your decrees (Psalm 119:68).

> Do not conform any longer to the pattern of this world, but be transformed by the renewing of your mind. Then you will

be able to test and approve what God's will is—his good, pleasing and perfect will (Romans 12:2).

And we know that in all things God works for the good of those who love him, who have been called according to his purpose (Romans 8:28-29).

If you, then, though you are evil, know how to give good gifts to your children, how much more will your Father in heaven give good gifts to those who ask him! (Matthew 7:11).

Be joyful always; pray continually; give thanks in all circumstances, for this is God's will for you in Christ Jesus (1 Thessalonians 5:16-18).

Now the question is, do you believe God's Word in the Bible? If you do, you have a "living hope" and "glorious joy" that even anxiety and depression cannot overcome:

Praise be to the God and Father of our Lord Jesus Christ! In his great mercy he has given us new birth into a living hope through the resurrection of Jesus Christ from the dead, and into an inheritance that can never perish, spoil or fade—kept in heaven for you, who through faith are shielded by God's power until the coming of the salvation that is ready to be revealed in the last time. In this you greatly rejoice, though now for a little while you may have had to suffer grief in all kinds of trials. These have come so that your faith—of greater worth than gold, which perishes even though refined by fire—may be proved genuine and may result in praise, glory and honor when Jesus Christ is revealed. Though you have not seen him, you love him; and even though you do not see him now, you believe in him and are filled with an inexpressible and glorious joy, for you are receiving the goal of your faith, the salvation of your souls (1 Peter 1:3-9).

Gold in the Fire

He sat by a fire of sevenfold heat,
As He watched by the precious ore,
And closer He bent with a searching gaze
As He heated it more and more.

He knew He had ore that could stand the test,
And He wanted the finest gold
To mold as a crown for the King to wear,
Set with gems with price untold.

So He laid our gold in the burning fire,
Tho' we fain would have said to Him, "Nay,"
And He watched the dross that we had not seen,
And it melted and passed away.

And the gold grew brighter and yet more bright,
But our eyes were so dim with tears.
We saw but the fire—not the Master's hand—
And questioned it with anxious fears.

Yet our gold shone out with a richer glow,
As it mirrored a Form above,
That bent o'er the fire, tho' unseen by us,
With a look of ineffable love.

Can we think that it pleases His loving heart
To cause us a moment's pain?
Ah, no! But He saw through the present cross
The bliss of eternal gain.

So He waited there with a watchful eye,
With a love that is strong and sure,
And His gold did not suffer a bit more heat,
Than was needed to make it pure.

AUTHOR UNKNOWN

Peter makes a staggering statement in 2 Peter 1:2-4. He suggests that God has given us everything we need for life and godliness.

> Grace and peace be yours in abundance through the knowledge of God and of Jesus our Lord.
>
> His divine power has given us everything we need for life and godliness through our knowledge of him who called us by his own glory and goodness. Through these he has given us his very great and precious promises, so that through them you

may participate in the divine nature and escape the corruption in the world caused by evil desires.

Do you really believe what Peter said? Does "everything we need for life" include the ability to overcome anxiety and depression? Of course it does.

One of the major components of anxiety is fear. One of the major components of depression is discouragement. The Bible addresses these thoughts clearly and repeatedly.

> Do not be afraid; do not be discouraged (Deuteronomy 1:21).
>
> Do not be afraid; do not be discouraged (Deuteronomy 31:8).
>
> Be strong and courageous. Do not be terrified; do not be discouraged, for the LORD your God will be with you wherever you go (Joshua 1:9).
>
> Do not be afraid; do not be discouraged (Joshua 8:1).
>
> Do not be afraid; do not be discouraged. Be strong and courageous (Joshua 10:25).
>
> Be strong and courageous. Do not be afraid or discouraged (1 Chronicles 22:13).
>
> Be strong and courageous, and do the work. Do not be afraid or discouraged, for the LORD God, my God, is with you. He will not fail you or forsake you (1 Chronicles 28:20).
>
> This is what the LORD says to you: "Do not be afraid or discouraged" (2 Chronicles 20:15).
>
> Do not be afraid; do not be discouraged (2 Chronicles 20:17).
>
> Be strong and courageous. Do not be afraid or discouraged (2 Chronicles 32:7).
>
> I ask you, therefore, not to be discouraged (Ephesians 3:2-13).

Knowing that God is with you wherever you go and in every circumstance can calm your anxiety and ease your depression. God is always with those who have received Christ. Jesus has suffered worse troubles than we could ever know or experience. You can trust in His sovereignty.

Hebrews 13:5 says, "Never will I leave you; never will I forsake you." This sentence is powerful in English, but it is even stronger in the Greek. The Amplified Bible gives a much clearer picture of the thought. "He [God] Himself has said, I will not in any way fail you nor give you up nor leave you without support. [I will] not, [I will] not, [I will] not in any degree leave you helpless nor forsake nor let [you] down (relax My hold on you)! [Assuredly not!]" Now that's sovereignty.

About 300 years ago, a French theologian named François Fenelon wrote some very helpful thoughts about how to view trials and suffering:

> If we were dead [to self], and our life were hid with Christ in God, we would no longer perceive those pains in spirit that now afflict us. We would not only bear bodily sufferings with composure, but also, spiritual affliction.

> By spiritual affliction, I mean trouble that is sent upon the soul and is not caused by its own actions. The disturbances created by a restless activity, however, in which the soul adds to the cross imposed by the hand of God, and burdens itself by an agitated resistance and unwillingness to suffer,—are only experienced because of the remaining life of self.

> If we recognize the hand of God and make no opposition in our will, we have comfort in our affliction. Happy, indeed, are these who can bear their suffering in the enjoyment of this simple peace and perfect submission to the will of God! Nothing so shortens and soothes our pains as this spirit of nonresistance.

> But we generally want to bargain with God. We would like at least to impose the limits and see the end of our sufferings. That same obstinate and hidden hold of life, which renders the cross necessary, causes us to reject it in part by a secret resistance that impairs its virtue. So we have to go over the same ground again and again. Because of this we suffer greatly, but to very little purpose.

I have a strong concern that many believers in Christ separate their spiritual faith from their mental health. They ignore the promises of God and the admonitions of Scripture. Their perception of psychology leaves

God out of the mental health picture. Christians often assume their bipolar disorder is an illness. They discuss their phobias and fears as if drugs and psychologists can help and the Bible can't. The god of chemical imbalance has replaced the God of the universe, who made man in all of his complexity. Don't be afraid to challenge the concept of mental illness. The Bible is still the ultimate answer for the moral and emotional conflicts and dysfunctions of society.

There is no question that people hurt emotionally. There is no argument that some mental problems seem beyond us. The science of psychology can be beneficial, but it has not found a greater hope than is found in the Word of God.

If you have been struggling with anxiety and depression, I encourage you to invest time and energy into prayer and Bible study. In the pages of Scripture, God can soothe the broken heart and mend the troubled spirit.

In 1895, Andrew Murray was in England suffering from a terribly painful back injury. He was staying with some friends, and one morning while he was eating his breakfast in his room, his hostess told him a woman wanted to talk with him. She was in great trouble and wanted to know if he had any advice for her. Mr. Murray handed the hostess a paper he had been writing on. He said, "Just give her this advice I'm writing down for myself. It may be that she'll find it helpful." On the piece of paper was the following note:

> In time of trouble, say first, "He brought me here. It is by His will I am in this strait place; in that I will rest." Next, "He will keep me here in His love and give me grace in this trial to behave as His child." Then say, "He will make the trial a blessing, teaching me lessons He intends me to learn, and working in me the grace He means to bestow." And last, say, "In His good time He can bring me out again. How, and when, He knows." Therefore say, "I am here by God's appointment, in His keeping, under His training, for His time."

Although the world is full of suffering, it is full also of the overcoming of it.

HELEN KELLER

Appendix

ENCOURAGEMENT *from* *the* BIBLE

❖

The Scriptures teach us the best way of living,
the noblest way of suffering, and the
most comfortable way of dying.

JOHN FLAVEL

ABORTION

Jeremiah 1:1-5
Psalm 139

ABUSIVE BEHAVIOR

Romans 12:10
Romans 12:18-19
1 Thessalonians 5:15
James 1:20

ACCOUNTABILITY

Joshua 7:1-15
Ecclesiastes 12:13-14
Romans 14:1-22

ADULTERY

Hosea 1:1-11
Matthew 5:27-32
Luke 16:18
John 8:1-11

ADVICE

Proverbs 1:1-9
Proverbs 6:20-24
Proverbs 10:1-21
Mark 10:17-31

AFFECTIONS

Proverbs 4:23-27

ALCOHOLISM

Proverbs 20:1
Proverbs 23:29-35
2 Peter 2:19

ANGER

Matthew 5:21-26
Ephesians 4:26-32
James 1:19-20

ANXIETY

Psalm 16:11
Psalm 37:1,7
Isaiah 41:10

ARGUMENTS

Proverbs 15:1-9
Proverbs 26:17-28
Philippians 2:14
Titus 3:1-11

ATTITUDE

Philippians 2:5-11
Philippians 4:4-9

BACKSLIDING

Deuteronomy 8:10-20
Luke 9:57-62
James 5:15-20

BELIEF

Romans 10:5-13
James 2:14-24

BEREAVEMENT

Deuteronomy 31:8
Psalm 23:1-6
Psalm 27:10
Psalm 119:50

BITTERNESS

Hebrews 12:14-17
1 John 3:11-24

CHOICES

Proverbs 1:1-19
Proverbs 13:1-16
Matthew 9:9-13

COMFORT

Job 16
Lamentations 3:21-26
2 Corinthians 1:3-11

COMPLAINING

Philippians 2:12-18

CONFIDENCE

Matthew 19:26
Acts 5:17-32

CONFLICTS

James 4:1-12

CONSCIENCE

Proverbs 28:13-18
Acts 23:1
Acts 24:16
1 Timothy 3:8-9
Hebrews 10:21-22
1 Peter 3:16

CRITICISM

Matthew 7:1-5
Luke 17:1-10
Galatians 5:13-26

DECEIT

Exodus 20:1-21

DEPRESSION

1 Kings 19:1-18
Psalm 42:1-11

DESIRES

Psalm 97:1-12

DESPAIR

Exodus 14:1-14
Psalm 40:1-17

DIFFICULTIES

Romans 8:28
2 Corinthians 4:17
Hebrews 12:7-11
Revelation 3:19

DISAPPOINTMENT

Psalm 43:5
Psalm 55:22
Psalm 126:6
John 14:27
2 Corinthians 4:8-10

DISCERNMENT

Matthew 7:6
James 1:2-8

DISCOURAGEMENT

Joshua 1:9
Psalm 27:14
1 Peter 1:3-9
1 John 5:14

DISHONESTY

Proverbs 20:23-30

DISOBEDIENCE

Genesis 3:1-24
1 Chronicles 13:1-14

DIVISIONS

1 Corinthians 4:6-13

DIVORCE & REMARRIAGE

Malachi 2:15-16
Matthew 19:8-9
1 Corinthians 7:10-15

DRINKING

Proverbs 23:29-35
Ephesians 5:18

ENCOURAGEMENT

1 Thessalonians 5:16-18
1 Peter 1:1-13

ENTHUSIASM

Colossians 3:18-25

ENVY

Deuteronomy 5:21
1 Kings 21:1-29

ETERNAL LIFE

Luke 18:18-30
John 3:1-21
John 6:60-71
John 17:1-26
1 John 5:1-13

FAULTS

Matthew 7:1-5
Ephesians 4:1-3; 5:1-2

FEAR

Joshua 1:1-18
Psalm 27:1
Psalm 56:11
Psalm 91:1-6
Psalm 121:1-8
Proverbs 29:25

FOOLISHNESS

Psalm 14:1-7
Proverbs 9:1-18
1 Corinthians 2:14-16

FORGIVENESS

Psalm 51:1-19
Matthew 6:5-15
Matthew 18:21-35
Romans 12:1-21
1 John 1:1-10

FRIENDSHIP

Proverbs 17:1-28
John 15:1-17

FRUSTRATION

Ephesians 6:1-4

GAMBLING

Proverbs 15:16
Proverbs 23:4-5
Luke 12:15
1 Timothy 6:9

GENTLENESS

James 3:1-18

GOSSIP

Exodus 23:1
Proverbs 25:18

GREED

James 4:1-3

GUILT

Psalm 32:1-2
Romans 8:1-17
Colossians 2:9-17
1 John 3:11-24

HABITS

1 John 3:4-9

HAPPINESS

Matthew 5:1-12
1 Timothy 6:6-10

HEAVEN

John 14:1-14
Colossians 3:1-3

HELL

Matthew 25:41-46

Romans 1:18-32

Revelation 20:1-15

HELP

Psalm 46:1-11

Galatians 6:1-10

HOMOSEXUALITY

Romans 1:18-27

1 Corinthians 6:9-11

1 Timothy 1:1-11

HOPE

Romans 5:1-11

1 Thessalonians 4:13-18

HURT

Psalm 55:22

Psalm 56:3-4

Psalm 121:1-8

1 Peter 5:7

IMMORALITY

1 Corinthians 6:1-20

Revelation 9:13-21

INDECISIVENESS

John 3:22-36

INFERIORITY

Psalm 86:13

Psalm 139:13-16

1 Corinthians 1:26-29

1 Peter 2:9-10

INSULT

Proverbs 12:1-28

INTEGRITY

Psalm 25:1-22

Luke 16:1-15

JEALOUSY

Romans 13:13-14

JUDGING

Matthew 7:1-6

1 Corinthians 5:12-13

KINDNESS

Luke 6:27-36

Colossians 3:1-17

LAZINESS

2 Thessalonians 3:6-15

2 Peter 3:1-18

LIFESTYLE

Matthew 5:1-12

1 Corinthians 9:1-27

2 Timothy 2:14-16

LONELINESS

Psalm 23:1-6

Isaiah 41:10

Matthew 28:20

Hebrews 13:5-6

LUST

Mark 7:20-23
Romans 6:12
1 Thessalonians 4:3-8
James 1:14-15

LYING

Proverbs 17:20
Proverbs 19:9
Proverbs 24:24
Proverbs 26:28
Proverbs 29:12
Matthew 5:37
Ephesians 4:25

MATERIALISM

Matthew 6:19-24

MORALITY

Romans 2:1-16
Romans 12:1-8

MOTIVES

Jeremiah 17:1-18
James 4:1-12

MURDER

Deuteronomy 5:17
James 4:1-12

OBEDIENCE

Deuteronomy 30:11-19

OCCULT

Deuteronomy 18:9-13

1 Samuel 28:7-12
2 Kings 21:6
Isaiah 47:13-14
Acts 19:18-20

PAIN

Hebrews 12:1-13

PEACE

Psalm 3:3-6
John 14:1
Romans 5:1-11

PRIORITIES

Proverbs 3
Matthew 6:25-34

PROBLEMS

James 1:1-18

PROCRASTINATION

Proverbs 10:1-32
Proverbs 26:13-16

QUARRELS

Proverbs 13:1-10
Titus 3:1-11
James 4:1-12

RELATIONSHIPS

2 Corinthians 6:14-18
Ephesians 2:11-22

REVENGE

Romans 12:17-21

RIGHTEOUSNESS

Psalm 51

SELF-CENTEREDNESS

Mark 8:31-38

1 Peter 1:14-25

SELFISHNESS

Mark 8:31-38

James 4:1-10

SEX

Proverbs 5:15-21

1 Corinthians 7:1-11

1 Thessalonians 4:1-8

SICKNESS

Psalm 41:3

Psalm 103:3

Matthew 4:23

John 11:4

James 5:13-15

SIN

Isaiah 53:5-6

Isaiah 59:1-2

John 8:34

Romans 3:23

Romans 6:23

Galatians 6:7-8

STRESS

Romans 5:1-5

Philippians 4:4-9

SUFFERING

Romans 8:18

2 Corinthians 1:5

Philippians 3:10

2 Timothy 2:12

James 1:2-8

1 Peter 1:6-7

SUICIDE

Job 14:5

Romans 14:7

1 Corinthians 6:19-20

TEMPTATION

Psalm 94:17-18

Proverbs 28:13

1 Corinthians 10:12-13

Hebrews 4:14-16

James 1:13-15

TERMINAL ILLNESS

Jeremiah 29:11

2 Corinthians 12:9

2 Timothy 2:12

THANKFULNESS

Psalm 92:1-15

Romans 1:18-23

UNPARDONABLE SIN

Matthew 12:31-32

Mark 3:28-29

WAITING

Psalm 27:1-14

Psalm 40:1-4
Matthew 24:32-51

WEAKNESSES

2 Corinthians 12:1-10
1 John 3:1-11

WILL OF GOD

Psalm 37:4
Psalm 91:1-2
Proverbs 3:5-6
Proverbs 4:26
Ephesians 5:15-21
Philippians 2:12-13
1 Thessalonians 4:3
1 Peter 3:17

WISDOM

Psalm 119:97-112
Proverbs 1:1-7
Ecclesiastes 8:1-8
Luke 2:33-40
James 1:2-8

WORRY

Psalm 37:1-11
Matthew 6:25-34
Philippians 4:4-9

Notes

❖

Chapter 6—The Discerning Mind

1. Joseph Glenmullen, *Prozac Backlash* (New York: Simon and Schuster, 2000), 141.

2. Ibid., 156-57.

3. Ibid., 209.

4. A.B. Curtiss, *Depression Is a Choice* (New York: Hyperion, 2000), 74.

Chapter 7—The Discriminating Mind

1. Joseph Glenmullen, *Prozac Backlash* (New York: Simon and Schuster, 2000), 16, 210.

2. Ibid., 202.

3. American Medical Association, *Essential Guide to Depression* (New York: Pocket Books, 1998), 65.

4. Glenmullen, *Prozac Backlash,* 197.

5. Ibid., 196.

6. Ibid., 34-36, 44.

7. Ibid., 38.

8. Ibid., 77.

9. Ibid., 120.

10. Ibid., 190.

11. Jay Adams, *Christ and Your Problems* (Nutley, NJ: Presbyterian and Reformed Publishing Company, 1971), 4.

Chapter 11—The Rescued Mind

1. Neil Nedley, *Depression, the Way Out* (Ardmore, OK: Nedley Publishing, 2001), 22, 27.

Chapter 12—The Revitalized Mind

1. A.B. Curtiss, *Depression Is a Choice* (New York: Hyperion, 2000), 68.

2. Milton Hammerly and Philip Leif Group, *Depression: The New Integrative Approach* (Avon, MA: Adams Media Corporation, 2001), 99.

3. Ibid., 291.

Bibliography

❖

Adams, Jay E. *Christ and Your Problems*. Nutley, New Jersey: Presbyterian and Reformed Publishing Company, 1971.

Adams, Jay E. *The Christian Counselor's Manual*. Phillipsburg, New Jersey: Presbyterian and Reformed Publishing Company, 1973.

Adams, Jay E. *Competent to Counsel*. Phillipsburg, New Jersey: Presbyterian and Reformed Publishing Company, 1970.

Adams, Jay E. *Coping with Counseling Crisis*. Grand Rapids: Baker Book House, 1976.

Adams, Lane. *How Come It Is Taking So Long to Get Better?* Wheaton, Illinois: Tyndale House Publishers, Inc., 1975.

Adams, Jay E. *How to Help People Change*. Grand Rapids: Zondervan Publishing Company, 1986.

Adams, Jay E. *Insight and Creativity in Christian Counseling*. Phillipsburg, New Jersey: Presbyterian and Reformed Publishing Company, 1982.

Adams, Jay E. *Update on Christian Counseling, vol. 1*. Grand Rapids: Baker Book House, 1980.

Adams, Jay E. *What About Nouthetic Counseling?* Grand Rapids: Baker Book House, 1976.

Adler, Alfred. *Understanding Human Nature*. New York: Fawcett Premier Books, 1927.

Ahlem, Lloyd H. *How to Cope with Conflict and Change*. Glendale, California: Regal Books, 1978.

Amen, Daniel G. *Healing Anxiety and Depression*. New York: G.P. Putnam's Sons, 2003.

American Medical Association. *Essential Guide to Depression*. New York: Pocket Books, 1998.

Anthony, Robert. *50 Ideas That Can Change Your Life!* New York: Berkley Books, 1982.

Augsburger, David. *When Enough Is Enough*. Ventura, California: Regal Books, 1984.

Backus, William. *Telling Each Other the Truth*. Minneapolis: Bethany House Publishers, 1985.

Baker, Don, and Nester, Emery. *Depression: Finding Hope and Meaning in Life's Darkest Shadow*. Portland, Oregon: Multnomah Press, 1983.

Barrett, Roger. *Depression: What It Is and What to Do About It.* Elgin, Illinois: David C. Cook Publishing Company, 1977.

Beck, Aaron T. *Depression: Causes and Treatment.* Philadelphia: University of Pennsylvania Press, 1967.

Beck, Aaron T. *Feeling Good.* New York: William Morrow and Company, Inc., 1980.

Bliss, Edwin. *Doing It Now.* New York: Bantam Books, 1983.

Bloch, Douglas. *Healing from Depression.* Berkeley, California: Celestial Arts, 2002.

Brande, Dorothea. *Wake Up and Live!* New York: Cornerstone Library, 1968.

Brandt, Henry. *When You're Tired of Treating the Symptoms, and You're Ready for a Cure, Give Me a Call.* Brentwood, Tennessee: Wolgemuth and Hyatt Publishers, Inc., 1991.

Broida, Marian. *New Hope for People with Depression.* New York: Three Rivers Press, 2001.

Brooks, Michael. *Instant Rapport.* New York: Warner Books, Inc., 1989.

Burns, David. *The Feeling Good Handbook.* New York: A Plume Book, 1989.

Cammer, Leonard. *Up from Depression.* New York: Pocket Books, 1969.

Carlson, Dwight L. *Living God's Will.* Old Tappan, New Jersey: Fleming H. Revell Company, 1976.

Carlson, Dwight, and Wood, Susan Carlson. *When Life Isn't Fair.* Eugene, Oregon: Harvest House Publishers, 1989.

Carter-Scott, Cherie. *Negaholics.* New York: Fawcett Crest, 1989.

Castle, Lana R. *Bipolar Disorder Demystified.* New York: Marlon & Company, 2003.

Chansky, Tamar E. *Freeing Your Child from Obsessive Compulsive Disorder.* New York: Three Rivers Press, 2000.

Collins, Gary R. *Christian Counseling.* Waco, Texas: Word Books, 1980.

Collins, Gary. *How to Be a People Helper.* Santa Ana, California: Vision House Publishers, 1976.

Cosgrove, Mark P. *Psychology Gone Awry.* Grand Rapids: Zondervan Publishing House, 1979.

Cousens, Gabriel. *Depression-Free for Life.* New York: Quill, 2000.

Crabb, Larry. *Effective Biblical Counseling.* Grand Rapids: Zondervan Publishing House, 1977.

Crabb, Larry. *Understanding People.* Grand Rapids: Zondervan Publishing House, 1987.

Curtiss, A.B. *Depression Is a Choice: Winning the Battle Without Drugs.* New York: Hyperion, 2001.

Dalbey, Gordon. *Healing the Masculine Soul.* Waco, Texas: Word Books, 1988.

Davis, Ron Lee. *The Healing Choice*. Waco, Texas: Word Books, 1986.

Demaray, Donald. *Laughter, Joy, and Healing*. Grand Rapids: Baker Book House, 1986.

Dickinson, Richard W., and Page, Carole Gift. *The Child in Each of Us*. Wheaton, Illinois: Victor Books, 1989.

Dobson, James. *Emotions: Can You Trust Them?* Ventura, California: Regal Books, 1980.

Dotts, Nancy. *Loneliness: Living Between the Times*. Wheaton, Illinois: Victor Books, 1978.

Dreikurs, Rudolf. *Fundamentals of Adlerian Psychology*. Chicago: Alfred Adler Institute, 1933.

Elliott, Charles H., and Smith, Laura L. *Overcoming Anxiety for Dummies*. New York: Wiley Publishing, 2003.

Ellis, Albert, and Harper, Robert A. *A Guide to Rational Living*. North Hollywood, California: Wilshire Book Company, 1961.

Evans, Stephen C. *Despair*. Downers Grove, Illinois: InterVarsity Press, 1971.

Ferguson, Ben. *God I've Got a Problem*. Santa Ana, California: Vision House, 1974.

Fisher, Roger, and Ury, William. *Getting to Yes*. New York: Penguin Books, 1981.

Frankl, Viktor E. *The Will to Meaning*. New York: Penguin Books, 1988.

Fronk, Ron L. *Creating a Lifestyle You Can Live With*. Springdale, Pennsylvania: Whitaker House, 1988.

Gardner, James, and Bell, Arthur H. *Overcoming Anxiety, Panic, and Depression*. Franklin Lakes, New Jersey: Career Press, 2000.

Gillespie, Peggy Roggenbuck, and Bechtel, Lynn. *Less Stress in 30 Days*. New York: Signet, 1987.

Girdano, Daniel, and Everly, George. *Controlling Stress and Tension*. Englewood Cliffs, New Jersey: Prentice-Hall, 1979.

Glasser, William. *Control Therapy*. New York: Harper and Row Publishers, 1985.

Glasser, William. *Mental Health or Mental Illness*. New York: Harper and Row Publishers, 1970.

Glasser, William. *Reality Therapy*. New York: Harper and Row Publishers, 1965.

Glenmullen, Joseph. *Prozac Backlash: Overcoming the Dangers of Prozac, Zoloft, Paxil and Other Antidepressants with Safe, Effective Alternatives*. New York: Simon & Schuster, 2000.

Goddard, Hazel B. *I've Got That Hopeless, Caged-In Feeling*. Wheaton, Illinois: Tyndale House Publishers, 1971.

Goodman, Gerald, and Esterly, Glenn. *The Talk Book*. New York: Ballantine Books, 1988.

Graham, Billy. *The Billy Graham Christian Worker's Handbook*. Minneapolis: World Wide Publications, 1981.

Greist, John H., and Jefferson, James W. *Depression and Its Treatment*. New York: Warner Books, 1984.

Haggai, John. *How to Win over Loneliness*. Nashville: Thomas Nelson Publishers, 1979.

Haggai, John. *How to Win over Worry*. Grand Rapids: Zondervan Publishing House, 1959.

Halper, Jan. *Quiet Desperation*. New York: Warner Books, 1988.

Hammerly, Milton. *Depression: The New Integrative Approach*. Avon, Massachusetts: Adams Media Corporation, 2001.

Hansel, Tim. *Eating Problems for Breakfast*. Dallas, Texas: Word Publishing, 1988.

Hanson, Peter G. *The Joy of Stress*. Kansas City, Kansas: Andrews and McMeel, 1987.

Hart, Archibald D. *Adrenaline and Stress*. Waco, Texas: Word Books, 1986.

Hart, Archibald D. *The Anxiety Cure*. Nashville: Thomas Nelson, 1999.

Hart, Archibald D. *Dark Clouds: Silver Linings*. Colorado Springs: Focus on the Family Publishing, 1993.

Hart, Archibald D. *Unlocking the Mystery of Your Emotions*. Dallas: Word Publishing, 1989.

Helmstetter, Shad. *Choices*. New York: Pocket Books, 1989.

Helton, Lonnie R., and Smith, Mieko K. *Mental Health Practice with Children and Youth*. New York: Haworth Social Work Practice Press, 2004.

Herink, Richie. *The Psychotherapy Handbook*. New York: A Meridian Book, 1980.

Hocker, Joyce, and Wilmot, William W. *Interpersonal Conflict*. Dubuque, Iowa: Wm. C. Brown Publishers, 1978.

Howard, Grant J. *Knowing God's Will and Doing It!* Grand Rapids: Zondervan Publishing House, 1976.

Hulme, William E. *Creative Loneliness*. Minneapolis: Augsburg Publishing House, 1977.

Jackson, Edgar. *Understanding Loneliness*. Philadelphia: Fortress Press, 1980.

Jauncey, James H. *Above Ourselves*. Grand Rapids: Zondervan Publishing House, 1964.

Jeremiah, David. *Overcoming Loneliness*. San Bernardino, California: Here's Life Publishers, Inc., 1983.

Johnston, J. Kirk. *When Counseling Is Not Enough*. Grand Rapids: Discovery House, 1994.

Jones, Brian G., and Phillips-Jones, Linda. *Men Have Feelings Too*. Wheaton, Illinois: Victor Books, 1988.

Katon, Wayne, Ludman, Evette, and Simon, Gregory. *The Depression Help Book*. Boulder, Colorado: Bull Publishing Company, 2002.

Keating, Paul. *Emotions and Mental Health*. New Canaan, Connecticut: Keats Publishing, Inc., 1975.

Kleinknecht, Ronald A. *Mastering Anxiety*. Cambridge, Massachusetts: Prenum Publishing Corporation, 1991.

Kramlinger, Keith. *Mayo Clinic on Depression*. Rochester, Minnesota: Mayo Clinic Trade Paper, 2001.

LaHaye, Tim. *How to Win Over Depression*. Grand Rapids: Zondervan Publishing House, 1974.

LaHaye, Tim, and Phillips, Bob. *Anger Is a Choice*. Grand Rapids: Zondervan Publishing House, 1982.

Leahy, Robert L., and Holland, Stephen J. *Treatment Plans and Interventions for Depression and Anxiety Disorders*. New York: The Guilford Press, 2000.

Lindquist, Stanley. *Action Helping Skills*. Fresno, California: Link-Care Foundation Press, 1976.

Losoncy, Lewis. *Turning People On*. New York: Prentice Hall Press, 1977.

Lum, Doman. *Responding to Suicidal Crisis*. Grand Rapids: William B. Eerdmans Publishing Company, 1977.

Lutzer, Erwin. *How to Say No to a Stubborn Habit*. Wheaton, Illinois: Victor Books, 1979.

Lutzer, Erwin. *Managing Your Emotions*. Chappaqua, New York: Christian Herald Books, 1981.

MacArthur, John. *God's Will Is Not Lost*. Wheaton, Illinois: Victor Books, 1973.

Mallory, James D. *The Kink and I*. Grand Rapids: Zondervan Publishing House, 1973.

Marsh, Peter. *Eye to Eye*. Topsfield, Massachusetts: Salem House Publishers, 1988.

Meillinger, David, and Lynn, Steven Jay. *The Monster in the Cave*. New York: Berkley Books, 2003.

Menninger, Karl. *Whatever Became of Sin?* New York: Hawthorn Books, 1973.

Miller, Sherod, et al. *Straight Talk*. New York: A Signet Book, 1981.

Minirth, Frank B., and Meier, Paul D. *Happiness Is a Choice*. Grand Rapids: Baker Book House, 1978.

Minirth, Frank B., Skipper, States V., and Meier, Paul D. *100 Ways to Defeat Depression*. Grand Rapids: Baker Book House, 1979.

Montgomery, Bob, and Morris, Laurel. *Living with Anxiety.* Cambridge, Massachusetts: Perseus Publishing, 2001.

Moorehead, Bob. *Counsel Yourself and Others from the Bible.* Sisters, Oregon: Questar Publishing, 1994.

Murphree, Jon Tal. *When God Says You're OK.* Downers Grove, Illinois: InterVarsity Press, 1976.

Nedley, Neil. *Depression: The Way Out.* Ardmore, Oklahoma: Nedley Publishing, 2001.

Neff, Miriam. *Women and Their Emotions.* Chicago: Moody Press, 1983.

Osborne, Cecil G. *Understanding Your Past: The Key to Your Future.* Waco, Texas: Word Books, 1980.

Perry, Lloyd M., and Sell, Charles M. *Speaking to Life's Problems.* Chicago: Moody Press, 1983.

Phillips, Bob. *42 Days to Feeling Great.* Eugene, Oregon: Harvest House, 2001.

Phillips, Bob. *What to Do Until The Psychiatrist Comes.* Eugene, Oregon: Harvest House, 1995.

Phillips, Bob, and Alyn, Kimberly. *How to Deal with Annoying People.* Eugene, Oregon: Harvest House, 2003.

Pokras, Sandy. *Systematic Problem Solving and Decision Making.* Los Altos, California: Crisp Publications, Inc., 1989.

Potthoff, Harvey H. *Understanding Loneliness.* New York: Harper and Row Publishers, 1976.

Reid, William H., and Wise, Michael G. *DSM-IV Training Guide.* New York: Brunner-Routledge, 1995.

Rohrer, Norman B., and Sutherland, S. Philip. *Why Am I Shy?* Minneapolis: Augsburg Publishing House, 1978.

Rosellini, Gayle, and Worden, Mark. *Of Course You're Anxious.* New York: HarperSan Francisco, 1990.

Rosen, Laura Epstein, and Amador, Xavier Francisco. *When Someone You Love Is Depressed.* New York: The Free Press, 1996.

Rubin, Theodore Isaac. *Overcoming Indecisiveness.* New York: Avon Books, 1985.

Salmans, Sandra. *Depression: Questions You Have…Answers You Need.* Allentown, Pennsylvania: People's Medical Society, 1995.

Schlenger, Sunny, and Roesch, Roberta. *How to Be Organized in Spite of Yourself.* New York: A Signet Book, 1989.

Schmidt, Kenneth. *Finding Your Way Home.* Ventura, California: Regal Books, 1990.

Scott, Gini Graham. *Resolving Conflict.* Oakland, California: New Harbinger Publications, Inc., 1990.

Sehnert, Keith W. *Stress and Unstress.* Minneapolis: Augsburg Publishing House, 1981.

Semands, David. *Healing for Damaged Emotions.* Wheaton, Illinois: Victor Books, 1981.

Smedes, Lewis B. *Forgive and Forget.* New York: Pocket Books, 1984.

Solomon, Andrew. *The Noonday Demon: An Atlas of Depression.* New York: Simon & Schuster, 2001.

Solomon, Charles R. *Counselling with the Mind of Christ.* Old Tappan, New Jersey: Fleming H. Revell Company, 1977.

Solomon, Charles R. *Handbook of Happiness.* Denver, Colorado: House of Solomon, 1971.

Steiner, Claude. *Scripts People Live.* New York: Bantam Books, 1974.

Szasz, Thomas. *A Lexicon of Lunacy.* New Brunswick, New Jersey: Transaction Publishers, 2003.

Szasz, Thomas. *Anti-Freud.* Syracuse, New York: Syracuse University Press, 1976.

Szasz, Thomas. *Insanity.* New York: John Wiley & Sons, 1987.

Szasz, Thomas S. *The Manufacture of Madness.* New York: Harper and Row Publishers, 1977.

Szasz, Thomas S. *The Myth of Mental Illness.* New York: Harper Colophon Books, 1974.

Szasz, Thomas. *The Myth of Psychotherapy.* Garden City, New York: Anchor Books, 1979.

Szasz, Thomas. *The Therapeutic State.* Buffalo, New York: Prometheus Books, 1984.

Torrey, E. Fuller, and Knable, Michael B. *Surviving Manic Depression.* New York: Perseus Books Group, 2002.

Vasey, Michael W. and Dadds, Mark R. *The Developmental Psychopathology of Anxiety.* New York: Oxford University Press, 2001.

Viscott, David. *The Language of Feelings.* New York: Pocket Books, 1976.

Viscott, David. *The Viscott Method.* New York: Pocket Books, 1984.

Von Oech, Roger. *A Kick in the Seat of the Pants.* New York: Harper and Row Publishers, 1986.

Von Oech, Roger. *A Whack in the Side of the Head.* New York: Harper and Row Publishers, 1983.

Wahlroos, Sven. *Excuses.* New York: Macmillan Publishing Company, Inc., 1981.

Walsh, Thomas A. *Beyond Psychology.* Eau Gallie, Florida: Harbour House, 1990.

Walters, Candace. *Invisible Wounds.* Portland, Oregon: Multnomah Press, 1987.

Whybrow, Peter, and Bahr, Robert. *The Hibernation Response*. New York: Avon Books, 1988.

Wood, Garth. *The Myth of Neurosis*. New York: Harper and Row Publishers, 1983.

Wright, Norman H. *The Christian Use of Emotional Power*. Old Tappan, New Jersey: Fleming H. Revell, 1974.

Yancey, Philip. *Where Is God When It Hurts?* Grand Rapids: Zondervan Publishing House, 1977.

Zimbardo, Philip G. *Shyness*. Reading, Massachusetts: Addison-Wesley Publishing Company, Inc., 1977.